QUICKBOOKS ONLINE

FOR SMALL BUSINESSES

A Step by Step Guide to Accounting, Invoicing, Expenses Tracking and Financial Reporting

CHAD SCOTT

Table of Content

Introduction

Welcome to *QuickBooks Online for Small Businesses*, a comprehensive guide crafted to help you navigate, utilize, and master one of the most powerful accounting tools available today. Whether you're a small business owner, a freelancer, or simply managing finances for your organization, QuickBooks Online (QBO) can simplify bookkeeping, increase financial transparency, and give you greater control over your finances. This book is designed to take you step-by-step through the fundamentals of QBO, from setup to advanced functionality, so you can confidently use it to manage your business or personal finances.

Overview of QuickBooks Online and Its Benefits

QuickBooks Online has become the go-to accounting software for millions of users worldwide, and for good reason. It offers a user-friendly, cloud-based platform that can be accessed from anywhere with an internet connection, providing flexibility and real-time financial insights. With QBO, you can easily track income and expenses, manage invoicing and payments, keep tabs on cash flow, and access detailed reports to understand the financial health of your business—all while ensuring accuracy and staying compliant with basic accounting principles.

One of the biggest advantages of QuickBooks Online is its scalability. The software is designed to grow with your business, offering a range of subscription options and a variety of integrations that allow you to customize the platform according to your needs. As your business grows, QBO can evolve with you, helping you automate repetitive tasks, streamline processes, and stay organized.

Moreover, QuickBooks Online uses powerful automation tools to simplify tasks such as invoicing, transaction categorization, and payroll. These features reduce the time spent on manual data entry, allowing you to focus on what truly matters—building and running a successful business.

Who This Book is For
This book is tailored for beginners who are either new to accounting software or new to QuickBooks Online specifically. It's ideal for:

- **Small Business Owners**: Whether you're running a startup, a family business, or a growing company, this book will guide you through using QBO to manage your day-to-day finances.
- **Freelancers and Solopreneurs**: If you work independently, QuickBooks Online can streamline your bookkeeping and help you keep track of income, expenses, and taxes. This book will show you how.

- **Bookkeepers and Accounting Students**: For those looking to enhance their knowledge of QBO, this guide serves as a solid foundation, covering core concepts and functionalities essential to bookkeeping.
- **Nonprofits and Community Organizations**: QuickBooks Online is also a great tool for organizations that need a straightforward, effective way to manage donations, track expenses, and maintain financial records.

Whether you have previous experience with accounting or are entirely new to the concept, *QuickBooks Online for Small Busine*sses will meet you where you are and build your confidence in managing finances with ease and accuracy.

How to Use This Book for Maximum Success
This book is structured to provide a clear, progressive path from QuickBooks Online's basics to its more advanced features. Each chapter is organized to build upon the previous one, introducing concepts and functions in a logical sequence. Here's how to get the most out of it:

1. **Follow the Chapters in Sequence**: To fully understand and utilize QBO, start with Part 1, which focuses on setting up your account and understanding foundational bookkeeping principles. As you progress through each part, you'll encounter more advanced functions and automation tips that build on earlier concepts.

2. **Practice with Real-World Examples**: Throughout the book, you'll find practical examples and case studies that demonstrate how QBO is used in different scenarios. These are included to reinforce the material and help you see how it applies to your unique situation. Try replicating these examples in your own QBO account to solidify your learning.
3. **Use the Bonus Materials**: At the end of the book, you'll find bonus materials like setup checklists, troubleshooting tips, and access to additional video tutorials. These resources are designed to support you beyond the pages of this book and provide practical tools you can refer to as you work in QuickBooks Online.
4. **Don't Be Afraid to Experiment**: QuickBooks Online is a dynamic tool, and the more you use it, the more comfortable you'll become. As you work through this book, spend time exploring different features in your own account to see how they might benefit your business or finances.
5. **Return to Chapters as Needed**: If you come across a chapter or concept that doesn't fully apply to your business now, don't worry—bookmark it and come back later. This book is intended to be a resource you can refer to as you grow and as your accounting needs evolve.

By the end of this book, you'll have the knowledge and skills to use QuickBooks Online confidently and efficiently. Not only will you understand the fundamentals of bookkeeping and accounting, but you'll also know how to leverage QBO's powerful features to save time, make better business decisions, and achieve your financial goals.

Let's get started on this journey to mastering QuickBooks Online!

Chapter 1

Setting Up Your QuickBooks Online Account

Before diving into the world of bookkeeping and financial management, it's essential to start with a solid foundation. This chapter will guide you through the process of setting up your QuickBooks Online (QBO) account, choosing the right subscription plan, and understanding the platform's key benefits. By the end, you'll be equipped with the essentials for a seamless experience in QuickBooks.

Overview and Benefits of QuickBooks Online

QuickBooks Online is a powerful, cloud-based accounting software developed to help individuals and businesses efficiently manage their finances. QBO offers a wide range of features that make bookkeeping accessible, even for those with minimal accounting experience. Here are some of the key benefits:

- **Accessibility Anywhere, Anytime**: Being cloud-based, QBO allows you to access your finances on any device with an internet connection. Whether you're at the office, at home, or on the go, you can manage your finances wherever you are.
- **Real-Time Financial Insights**: With QuickBooks Online, your financial data is always up-to-date. Bank account integrations and live transaction imports mean that you can get a clear view of your cash flow, income, and expenses in real time.
- **Automation Features**: QBO offers several automation tools that reduce manual work, such as automatic categorization of transactions, recurring invoices, and bank reconciliation tools. These features can save you valuable time and minimize errors.
- **Scalability**: Whether you're a freelancer, a small business owner, or managing multiple locations, QuickBooks Online has options to scale with your needs. As your business grows, QBO can adapt, offering more advanced functionalities and integrations.
- **Built-In Reporting and Compliance**: From standard financial statements to custom reports, QBO simplifies the reporting process. Additionally, QuickBooks Online is regularly updated to help users stay compliant with tax and regulatory changes, reducing risk and simplifying year-end reporting.

Choosing the Right QuickBooks Plan

QuickBooks Online offers several subscription plans to meet a range of business needs. It's important to select the plan that best suits your current requirements while considering potential future growth. Here's a quick breakdown of the main options:

1. **Simple Start**: This entry-level plan is ideal for freelancers, solopreneurs, and very small businesses. It allows users to track income and expenses, create and send invoices, capture and organize receipts, and run basic reports. Simple Start is best if you're just starting and need to get a handle on core bookkeeping.
2. **Essentials**: The Essentials plan includes all the features of Simple Start, with added benefits like managing bills and handling multiple users (up to 3). This plan is a good fit if your business has a bit more complexity, such as tracking vendor payments or managing a small team of users.
3. **Plus**: Designed for growing businesses, the Plus plan allows for up to 5 users and introduces features for inventory tracking, job costing, and project management. If you have more intricate needs, like tracking profitability by project or managing a small inventory, Plus could be the right choice.
4. **Advanced**: For larger businesses with complex needs, the Advanced plan offers up to 25 users, advanced reporting, and dedicated support. This plan includes features like custom workflows, advanced automation options, and detailed

analytics, making it suitable for companies with a high volume of transactions or unique reporting requirements.

Take some time to assess your business's needs carefully. If you're just beginning, it might be wise to start with a lower-tier plan and upgrade as your requirements expand.

Step-by-Step Guide to Setting Up Your Account

Once you've selected your plan, you're ready to set up your QuickBooks Online account. Follow these steps to get started:

Step 1: Sign Up for QuickBooks Online

1. Go to the QuickBooks Online website and click on the "Sign Up" button.
2. Select the plan that best fits your business needs and complete the purchase process.
3. After purchase, you'll be prompted to create a login and set up your primary account.

Step 2: Enter Basic Company Information

1. After signing in, QuickBooks Online will ask for basic information about your company, such as:
   - **Company Name**
   - **Industry**: Select your business type; this helps QBO suggest relevant features and setup options.

- **Company Address**: Used for invoices and other official documents.
2. You may also be asked about your preferred accounting method (Cash or Accrual) during setup. If you're unsure, select Cash (most small businesses operate on this basis) and consult an accountant if necessary.

Step 3: Customize Company Settings

1. Navigate to the **Settings** icon (gear icon) in the top right corner.
2. Under **Account and Settings**, customize your preferences, including:
    - **Company Name and Contact Information**: Ensure this matches your business registration.
    - **Sales Settings**: Choose options for sales forms like invoices, sales receipts, and credit memos.
    - **Expense Settings**: Set defaults for purchase orders, bills, and expense tracking.
    - **Tax Settings**: Input sales tax information if applicable, which will enable QuickBooks Online to calculate sales tax on your transactions.

Step 4: Set Up Your Chart of Accounts

1. Under **Accounting** in the left-hand menu, go to **Chart of Accounts**. QuickBooks Online will generate a basic chart of accounts based on your

business type, but you may want to add or edit accounts to better suit your needs.

2. For each account, specify the account type and detail type (e.g., Bank, Accounts Receivable). Use categories that align with your business for clear and accurate tracking.

3. If you're unsure about setting up the Chart of Accounts, review the next chapter, which covers this in detail.

Step 5: Connect Your Bank and Credit Card Accounts

1. In the left-hand menu, select **Banking**, and click on **Link Account**.

2. Enter your bank's login credentials to link your business accounts to QuickBooks Online. This will allow automatic importing of transactions, making it easier to keep your books current.

3. Once connected, review and categorize imported transactions to ensure accuracy.

Step 6: Set Up Users and Permissions

1. If you have additional team members who need access, go to **Settings > Manage Users** and add them.

2. Set appropriate permissions for each user based on their role. For example, you may want to restrict access to financial reports or payroll for some team members.

Step 7: Customize Invoices and Sales Forms

1. Under **Settings** > **Custom Form Styles**, you can design invoices, estimates, and sales receipts.
2. Customize these forms with your logo, preferred colors, and company details to maintain a professional, branded look.

Step 8: Explore Essential Features

Take a few moments to explore the core features of QuickBooks Online. This includes **Invoicing**, **Expense Tracking**, and **Reporting** sections, which are central to day-to-day financial management. Familiarizing yourself with the layout will make your workflow more intuitive as you move forward.

Setting up your QuickBooks Online account is a key first step toward organized, efficient bookkeeping. With your account configured, you're ready to dive into core bookkeeping functions, which we'll cover in the next chapters. Taking the time to set up your account accurately from the start will ensure smooth, accurate financial tracking and set you up for long-term success with QuickBooks Online.

Chapter 2

Navigating the Dashboard and Customizing Settings

Getting comfortable with the QuickBooks Online dashboard is essential for efficiently managing your financial tasks. The dashboard serves as your control center, providing an at-a-glance view of key financial metrics. In this chapter, we'll cover how to navigate the dashboard, customize views to suit your business needs, and adjust company settings for seamless operation. We'll finish with a practical example on how to tailor QuickBooks for a specific business.

Understanding the Dashboard

When you first log into QuickBooks Online, the dashboard is the landing page you'll see. It's designed to give you a quick summary of your business's financial health and recent activities. Let's break down its main sections:

1. Overview Panel

- This top section of the dashboard provides a snapshot of your financials, including cash flow, income, expenses, and profit and loss.

- Here, you can quickly see which areas might need your attention, such as overdue invoices or outstanding bills.

2. Cash Flow

- The Cash Flow widget offers a real-time view of your available cash and projected cash flow.
- This can help you anticipate upcoming expenses and ensure your business stays financially stable.

3. Income and Expense Overview

- This section presents a breakdown of your income and expenses over time. You can customize the time period (e.g., weekly, monthly, quarterly) for more detailed insights.
- Clicking on each component will take you to detailed reports, where you can drill down into specific transactions.

4. Bank Accounts

- The Bank Accounts widget lists your connected accounts and their current balances, with a status indicator for reconciliations.
- Clicking on an account here will take you to the transaction feed, where you can review and categorize expenses.

5. Profit and Loss

- The Profit and Loss widget displays your income, cost of goods sold, and expenses, giving you a quick glance at your net income.
- You can adjust the period to match your reporting needs, such as monthly or quarterly, and export the data for more detailed analysis.

6. Invoices and Expenses

- Quick access to recent invoices, along with their payment status, and a similar section for expenses. This helps you manage cash flow by keeping track of incoming and outgoing funds.

Customizing Views and Setting Up Company Preferences

Customizing the dashboard and setting up company preferences are crucial steps for tailoring QuickBooks Online to your business. Adjusting the layout and visibility of various components makes it easier to access the information you use most frequently, while company settings allow you to establish how financial data is tracked, displayed, and reported.

1. Customizing the Dashboard View

- You can rearrange and hide sections on the dashboard to highlight the areas that matter most. For example, if cash flow is your primary focus, ensure it's prominently displayed.

- To adjust a widget, click on the gear icon in the dashboard's top-right corner. Here, you'll find options to show or hide specific widgets.

2. Setting Up Company Preferences

- **Company Information**: Access the Settings menu (gear icon) > Account and Settings. Here, you can add or edit your business name, address, phone number, and tax information. This information will automatically populate on invoices and reports.
- **Sales Preferences**: Customize how you manage sales by setting default terms, email templates, and discounts. You can also select options to track inventory or use sales tax based on your business needs.
- **Expenses Preferences**: Under the Expenses tab, enable purchase orders if applicable and set a default bill payment term.
- **Payments and Banking**: Set up your preferred methods of receiving payments, whether through bank transfers, credit cards, or other gateways. For bank feeds, configure automatic transaction import settings.
- **Advanced Settings**: In the Advanced tab, you'll find options for setting your fiscal year, accounting method, and other financial controls.

3. Creating Custom Fields

- QuickBooks allows you to create custom fields for tracking specific information relevant to your business. For example, you could add a "Project" field to invoices if you frequently bill by project.
- To add custom fields, go to the Settings menu > Custom Form Styles, and select which forms the fields should appear on (e.g., invoices, estimates).

4. Setting Up Notifications and Alerts

- QuickBooks Online offers notification settings that alert you to critical activities, like overdue invoices, upcoming bills, or low inventory levels.
- You can manage these alerts in the Settings > Notifications section and choose whether they're sent via email, in-app, or both.

Practical Example

Tailoring QuickBooks for Your Business
To see how customization works in practice, let's walk through a practical example: setting up QuickBooks Online for a freelance graphic designer.

Scenario: Jamie runs a freelance graphic design business, offering services like logo design, website graphics, and social media branding. Jamie needs QuickBooks to manage invoicing, track project expenses, and handle monthly cash flow reports.

Step 1: Customizing Invoices with Branding

- Jamie navigates to the Settings menu > Custom Form Styles to create a personalized invoice template.
- She uploads her business logo, chooses a color scheme that aligns with her brand, and customizes the invoice fields to include "Project Name."

Step 2: Adding a Custom Field for Projects

- To better organize income and expenses by project, Jamie adds a custom field labeled "Project" in the invoice settings. This field will now appear on all invoices, allowing her to filter transactions by project in reports.

Step 3: Setting Up Recurring Expenses

- Jamie has several recurring expenses, like software subscriptions and design tools. She sets these up under Expenses > Recurring Transactions to save time and automate entries.

Step 4: Configuring Project Tracking

- Under Settings > Advanced > Categories, Jamie enables the "Projects" feature, allowing her to track income and expenses by project.
- She can now create separate projects for each client or design job, giving her clear visibility into each project's profitability.

Step 5: Establishing Monthly Cash Flow Alerts

- To stay on top of her cash flow, Jamie sets up monthly notifications that summarize her cash position and alert her of any overdue invoices.
- In the Settings > Notifications section, she configures the alerts to be delivered via email, ensuring she won't miss any critical updates.

Step 6: Customizing Reports for Clients

- Jamie frequently needs to show clients the progress of work, so she customizes the Profit and Loss and Expense reports to be filtered by project.
- This way, she can provide clients with a report showing only the financial details relevant to their project.

By setting up QuickBooks Online with customized views and preferences, you're equipping your business with a powerful, tailored tool for financial management. Take the time to configure these settings thoughtfully; they'll save time, reduce errors, and provide a clearer picture of your finances in the long run.

Chapter 3

Setting Up Your Chart of Accounts

Setting up your Chart of Accounts (COA) in QuickBooks Online is a foundational step in managing your financials accurately. The COA organizes every aspect of your business's finances, from income and expenses to assets and liabilities, allowing you to keep track of transactions, understand your financial position, and generate reliable reports. This chapter will guide you through defining accounts, establishing accounting conventions, creating and managing lists, and avoiding common pitfalls in COA setup.

Defining Accounts and Establishing Accounting Conventions

The Chart of Accounts is essentially a roadmap of all financial accounts used by your business. Each account in the COA falls into one of five primary categories:

1. **Assets** – Things of value that your business owns, such as cash, equipment, and accounts receivable.
2. **Liabilities** – Obligations your business owes to others, like loans or accounts payable.
3. **Equity** – The owner's stake in the business, including capital and retained earnings.

4. **Income (Revenue)** – Money your business earns from its main operations, like sales or services.
5. **Expenses** – Costs your business incurs to generate income, such as rent, utilities, and supplies.

QuickBooks Online provides predefined account types under each of these categories. While these account types generally suit most small businesses, it's essential to customize them according to your specific business needs.

Establishing Accounting Conventions

To ensure consistency and clarity in financial reporting, it's critical to establish accounting conventions when setting up your COA:

- **Naming Conventions**: Choose clear, consistent names for accounts. For example, instead of vague labels like "Miscellaneous Expenses," use specific terms like "Office Supplies" or "Travel Expenses."
- **Numbering System**: Some businesses use a numbering system to organize accounts. For example, you might assign "1000" series numbers to assets, "2000" to liabilities, and so forth. Numbering helps locate and categorize accounts quickly, especially in larger COAs.
- **Hierarchy**: QuickBooks Online allows you to create sub-accounts, which can help organize and summarize similar accounts. For example, under the primary "Expenses" account, you

could have sub-accounts like "Marketing," "Payroll," and "Utilities."

Creating and Managing Lists

QuickBooks Online makes it simple to create and manage your COA. Here's a step-by-step guide to setting up and organizing your list of accounts:

1. **Accessing the Chart of Accounts**:
   - In QuickBooks Online, go to **Settings** (gear icon) > **Chart of Accounts**.
   - Here, you'll see a list of predefined accounts, which you can edit, delete, or add to according to your needs.
2. **Adding New Accounts**:
   - Click **New** to create an account.
   - Choose the **Account Type** (e.g., Income, Expense, Asset) and **Detail Type** (e.g., Rent Expense, Equipment).
   - Give your account a descriptive **Name** and, if needed, an **Account Number** based on your numbering convention.
   - You can also add a brief **Description** to clarify the account's purpose.
3. **Creating Sub-Accounts**:
   - Sub-accounts help you categorize similar accounts. For instance, under "Marketing Expenses," you might have sub-accounts for "Online Advertising" and "Print Media."
   - When adding a new account, simply check the box for **Is sub-account** and select the parent account.

4. **Editing and Deleting Accounts**:
   - To modify an existing account, click the **Edit** button beside it in the Chart of Accounts. Update the details as needed.
   - If an account is no longer needed, you can make it inactive by clicking **Delete** (this won't delete the historical transactions tied to the account; they'll remain in your records).
5. **Merging Duplicate Accounts**:
   - If you accidentally create two accounts for the same purpose (e.g., "Advertising" and "Ads"), you can merge them to avoid redundancy.
   - To merge, edit one account's name to exactly match the other, then save it. QuickBooks will prompt you to confirm the merge.

Common Pitfalls in Chart of Accounts Setup
Setting up your COA thoughtfully is crucial to avoid future headaches. Below are some common pitfalls to watch out for:

1. **Overloading with Too Many Accounts**:
   - While it's tempting to create detailed accounts for every expense, having too many accounts can lead to clutter and complexity. Stick to the essential accounts you need to understand your finances.
   - Use sub-accounts for further detail only if necessary, as over-categorization can make financial reports harder to read and interpret.

2. **Vague Account Naming**:
   - Ambiguous names can lead to misclassified transactions and confusion. For instance, instead of "Miscellaneous Income," specify categories such as "Consulting Income" or "Product Sales."
   - Clear, specific naming ensures that all transactions are accurately classified and easily understood.
3. **Ignoring Regular Updates**:
   - As your business evolves, your COA should adapt. Set a routine for reviewing and updating your accounts periodically.
   - For example, if your business begins a new revenue stream, create an appropriate income account rather than lumping it into a catch-all category.
4. **Not Using Sub-Accounts Effectively**:
   - Failing to use sub-accounts for grouped transactions can lead to reporting issues. For example, grouping "Marketing" expenses (like "Social Media Ads" and "Print Ads") under a single "Marketing" category simplifies reporting.
   - However, avoid creating excessive layers of sub-accounts, as it can make data entry cumbersome and your reports overly complex.
5. **Overlooking Account Numbering**:
   - Using a logical numbering system can greatly simplify locating and categorizing accounts, especially if your COA grows over time.

- Many businesses skip this step initially, only to face challenges later when they need better organization. It's wise to establish a numbering structure from the start if you foresee growth.

6. **Duplicating Accounts by Accident**:
   - Duplicate accounts (such as "Advertising Expense" and "Marketing Expense") can lead to misclassification. Review the COA regularly to merge any duplicates and maintain accuracy.

By setting up a well-organized Chart of Accounts, you'll create a solid foundation for your business's financial management. Investing time upfront in defining accounts, establishing conventions, and maintaining the COA will save you time, reduce errors, and make financial tracking much smoother as your business grows.

Chapter 4

Essential Bookkeeping Concepts for QuickBooks Users

Effective bookkeeping is the backbone of any successful business. Understanding key bookkeeping concepts and adhering to best practices ensures that your financial records are accurate, organized, and compliant with regulatory standards. This chapter will cover the fundamental financial statements, essential accounting principles, and best practices tailored for beginners. Additionally, we'll provide a practical example to help you set up your bookkeeping system for long-term success.

Understanding Financial Statements and Key Accounting Principles

Financial statements are vital tools that provide insights into your business's financial health. They summarize your financial activities, helping you make informed decisions, secure financing, and comply with tax obligations. Here, we'll explore the three primary financial statements and the key accounting principles that underpin them.

1. The Three Primary Financial Statements

a. Profit and Loss Statement (Income Statement)

The Profit and Loss (P&L) Statement, also known as the Income Statement, summarizes your revenues, costs, and expenses over a specific period. It shows whether your business is profitable by calculating the net income.

Key Components:

- **Revenue (Sales):** Total income from goods sold or services provided.
- **Cost of Goods Sold (COGS):** Direct costs attributable to the production of goods sold.
- **Gross Profit:** Revenue minus COGS.
- **Operating Expenses:** Indirect costs such as rent, utilities, and salaries.
- **Net Income:** Gross profit minus operating expenses, taxes, and interest.

b. Balance Sheet

The Balance Sheet provides a snapshot of your business's financial position at a specific point in time. It lists your assets, liabilities, and equity, illustrating what your business owns and owes.

Key Components:

- **Assets:** Resources owned by the business (e.g., cash, inventory, equipment).
- **Liabilities:** Obligations owed to others (e.g., loans, accounts payable).
- **Equity:** Owner's interest in the business (e.g., retained earnings, capital).

c. Cash Flow Statement

The Cash Flow Statement tracks the flow of cash in and out of your business over a period. It helps you understand how well your business generates cash to meet its obligations.

Key Components:

- **Operating Activities:** Cash generated or used in core business operations.
- **Investing Activities:** Cash used for investing in assets or received from the sale of assets.
- **Financing Activities:** Cash received from or paid to investors and creditors.

2. Key Accounting Principles

Understanding and applying fundamental accounting principles ensures consistency and accuracy in your financial reporting. Here are the most important ones:

a. Accrual Basis vs. Cash Basis Accounting

- **Accrual Basis:** Records revenues and expenses when they are earned or incurred, regardless of when cash is exchanged. This method provides a more accurate picture of financial performance.
- **Cash Basis:** Records revenues and expenses only when cash is received or paid. This method is simpler but may not provide a complete view of financial health.

b. Double-Entry Accounting

Double-entry accounting requires that every financial transaction affects at least two accounts, maintaining the accounting equation: Assets = Liabilities + Equity. This system helps ensure the accuracy and balance of your books.

c. Consistency Principle

The consistency principle dictates that you should use the same accounting methods and procedures from period to period unless a change is warranted and justified. This allows for meaningful comparisons over time.

d. Prudence Principle

The prudence principle advises caution in financial reporting. It ensures that revenues and profits are not overstated and that liabilities and expenses are not understated.

e. Matching Principle

The matching principle requires that expenses be recorded in the same period as the revenues they help generate. This provides a clearer picture of profitability.

Bookkeeping Best Practices for Beginners

Adhering to best practices in bookkeeping helps maintain accurate financial records, reduces errors, and ensures compliance with regulations. Here are essential best practices to follow:

1. Keep Personal and Business Finances Separate

Maintaining separate accounts for personal and business finances prevents confusion and ensures that your business records accurately reflect its financial activities. Open a dedicated business bank account and use it exclusively for business transactions.

2. Stay Organized with a Consistent Filing System

Organize your financial documents systematically. Whether you prefer digital or physical filing, ensure that all receipts, invoices, bank statements, and financial reports are categorized and easily accessible.

3. Record Transactions Promptly

Timely recording of transactions helps prevent errors and ensures that your financial data is up-to-date. Set aside regular time each day or week to enter transactions into QuickBooks Online.

4. Reconcile Bank Statements Regularly

Regular reconciliation of your bank statements with your QuickBooks records ensures that your books are accurate and free of discrepancies. Aim to reconcile at least monthly to catch and correct errors promptly.

5. Use Clear and Consistent Account Naming

Use descriptive and consistent names for your accounts to make it easier to categorize and understand your financial data. Avoid vague terms and ensure that each account name clearly reflects its purpose.

6. Leverage QuickBooks Online Features

Take full advantage of QuickBooks Online's features, such as automation tools, bank feeds, and reporting capabilities. These tools can save time, reduce manual entry, and enhance the accuracy of your bookkeeping.

7. Monitor and Review Financial Reports Regularly

Regularly review your financial statements to monitor your business's performance and make informed decisions. Set aside time each month to analyze key metrics and identify trends or areas needing attention.

8. Backup Your Data

Ensure that your financial data is backed up regularly to prevent loss due to technical issues or unforeseen events. QuickBooks Online automatically backs up your data, but it's wise to export and store copies periodically.

9. Seek Professional Advice When Needed

Don't hesitate to consult with an accountant or bookkeeper if you encounter complex financial issues or need assistance with tax compliance. Professional guidance can help you navigate challenges and optimize your financial management.

Practical Example

Setting Up for Success with Clear Bookkeeping Basics

To illustrate how these concepts and best practices come together, let's walk through a practical example of setting up bookkeeping for a new small business using QuickBooks Online.

Scenario: Emma's Handmade Jewelry Business

Emma has started a small business selling handmade jewelry online. She needs to set up her bookkeeping system to manage her finances, track sales, handle expenses, and prepare for tax season.

Step 1: Define Financial Accounts

Emma begins by setting up her Chart of Accounts in QuickBooks Online, ensuring she covers all necessary categories:

- **Assets:**
  - Bank Account
  - Inventory
  - Equipment (e.g., crafting tools)
- **Liabilities:**
  - Credit Card Payable
  - Loans
- **Equity:**
  - Owner's Capital
  - Retained Earnings
- **Income:**
  - Jewelry Sales
  - Custom Orders
- **Expenses:**
  - Materials (e.g., beads, wires)
  - Shipping Costs
  - Marketing and Advertising
  - Rent (for workspace)
  - Utilities

Step 2: Separate Business and Personal Finances

Emma opens a dedicated business bank account and credit card to keep her business transactions separate from her personal finances. This separation simplifies bookkeeping and ensures clarity in financial reporting.

Step 3: Organize Financial Documents

Emma sets up a digital filing system on her computer and cloud storage. She creates folders for:

- Invoices and Receipts
- Bank Statements
- Vendor Contracts
- Tax Documents

Step 4: Record Transactions Regularly

Emma commits to entering all sales, expenses, and transactions into QuickBooks Online daily. She uses QuickBooks' mobile app to capture and upload receipts instantly.

Step 5: Reconcile Bank Statements Monthly

At the end of each month, Emma reconciles her bank statements with QuickBooks Online to ensure that all transactions are accurately recorded and any discrepancies are addressed.

Step 6: Customize Invoicing and Reports

Emma customizes her invoice templates with her business logo and selects the appropriate fields to capture customer information and order details. She also sets up regular financial reports, such as P&L statements and cash flow reports, to monitor her business's performance.

Step 7: Utilize QuickBooks Automation Features

Emma sets up recurring invoices for regular customers and automates expense categorization to save time and reduce manual data entry. She also connects her online store to QuickBooks Online to automatically import sales transactions.

Step 8: Review and Adjust

Each quarter, Emma reviews her financial reports to assess her business's profitability and cash flow. She adjusts her budgeting and spending based on these insights to ensure sustainable growth.

Outcome:

By following these bookkeeping basics and best practices, Emma successfully maintains accurate financial records, gains valuable insights into her business's performance, and prepares effectively for tax season. Her organized and efficient bookkeeping system allows her to focus more on creating and selling beautiful jewelry, knowing that her finances are well-managed.

By understanding these essential bookkeeping concepts and implementing best practices, you lay a strong foundation for accurate financial management. Clear and organized bookkeeping not only keeps your business compliant but also empowers you with the information needed to drive informed decisions and foster growth. In the next chapter, we will delve into core bookkeeping functions, where you will learn how to manage invoices, track expenses, and reconcile bank accounts effectively using QuickBooks Online.

Chapter 5

Invoicing and Sales Management

Effectively managing invoices and sales is crucial for tracking revenue, managing cash flow, and maintaining customer relationships. QuickBooks Online offers powerful tools for creating invoices, managing sales receipts, and organizing customer data, which helps streamline your sales process and improve overall cash flow. This chapter will guide you through creating invoices and sales receipts, managing customer and job data, and offer a practical case study on how quick invoicing practices can positively impact cash flow.

Creating Invoices and Sales Receipts

Invoices and sales receipts are two essential documents for recording sales in QuickBooks Online. Understanding the difference and knowing when to use each is critical for accurate record-keeping.

1. Understanding Invoices vs. Sales Receipts

Invoices are typically used for sales made on credit, where the customer has an agreed-upon period to pay (e.g., net 30 days). When you send an invoice, you're essentially giving the customer a bill, which will reflect as Accounts Receivable in your books until it's paid.

Sales Receipts are used for immediate payments, such as in-person or online sales where the customer pays on the spot. Sales receipts are recorded as revenue immediately, bypassing Accounts Receivable.

2. Step-by-Step: Creating an Invoice in QuickBooks Online

Creating an invoice in QuickBooks Online is straightforward. Here's how:

1. **Navigate to the Sales Tab**: From the QuickBooks dashboard, click on "Sales" and select "Invoices."
2. **Click on New Invoice**: Click the "New Invoice" button to create a fresh invoice.
3. **Enter Customer Information**: Select an existing customer from the dropdown menu or add a new customer. QuickBooks Online allows you to input details like billing address, email, and contact information.
4. **Fill in Invoice Details**:
   - **Invoice Date**: The date the invoice is created.
   - **Due Date**: Select the due date based on your payment terms (e.g., net 15, net 30).
5. **Add Line Items**: Under the "Product/Service" column, select items from your product list or add new products/services.

- ○ **Description**: Briefly describe each item for clarity.
- ○ **Quantity**: Enter the number of units.
- ○ **Rate**: Enter the price per unit.
6. **Apply Discounts or Taxes**: QuickBooks enables you to apply discounts or taxes automatically based on pre-set tax rules.
7. **Review and Save**: Review all details for accuracy, then save and send the invoice directly to your customer via email, or print a physical copy if preferred.

3. Step-by-Step: Creating a Sales Receipt in QuickBooks Online

For customers who pay immediately, you'll use a sales receipt:

1. **Navigate to Sales Receipts**: Under the "Sales" tab, select "Sales Receipts."
2. **Click on New Sales Receipt**: Start a new receipt.
3. **Enter Customer Information**: As with invoices, you can select or add a customer.
4. **Add Products/Services**: Enter items the customer is purchasing, similar to how you'd add them to an invoice.
5. **Enter Payment Details**: Select the payment method (e.g., cash, credit card, check).
6. **Review and Save**: After confirming the information, save and issue the receipt.

Managing Customers, Jobs, and Sales Transactions

Keeping track of customers and the details associated with sales transactions is essential for a smooth sales process. QuickBooks Online has a robust Customer Center where you can store customer data, track outstanding balances, and monitor job progress.

1. Organizing Customer Data

Maintaining detailed customer records allows you to personalize interactions and follow up on outstanding payments. Here's how to manage customer data effectively in QuickBooks Online:

- **Add New Customers**: Under "Sales," go to "Customers" and click "New Customer" to input contact information, payment terms, and any other relevant data.
- **Customer Notes**: Add notes for specific details like payment preferences or special discounts.
- **Track Outstanding Balances**: QuickBooks automatically calculates each customer's balance, so you can quickly see which invoices are overdue.

2. Creating Jobs (Projects) for Customers

If you work on projects or jobs for clients, QuickBooks Online allows you to manage each job separately under the same customer. This feature is useful for businesses that provide ongoing services or work on a project-by-project basis.

1. **Go to Customers**: Under the "Sales" tab, select "Customers."
2. **Add New Project**: Choose a customer, then click "New Project" to create a separate job under that customer's profile.
3. **Track Progress and Costs**: You can track time and expenses for each job, making it easier to bill clients accurately and monitor project profitability.

3. Managing Sales Transactions

QuickBooks Online makes it easy to view, edit, or update sales transactions as needed. Under "Sales," you can view all invoices, sales receipts, and payments, allowing you to stay on top of your receivables.

Case Study

Improving Cash Flow with Quick Invoicing Practices

Cash flow is essential to any business, and slow invoicing practices can lead to delays in payment. By implementing efficient invoicing practices, you can reduce outstanding receivables, improve cash flow, and strengthen customer relationships. Here's a case study illustrating how a small consulting firm optimized cash flow through timely invoicing.

Scenario: Sarah runs a small marketing consulting firm. Her typical payment terms are net 30, but clients often delay payments beyond that period. Sarah realized that delayed invoicing was a key issue affecting her cash flow. She decided to streamline her invoicing process using QuickBooks Online.

Steps Taken:

1. **Automated Invoicing**: Sarah set up QuickBooks Online to automatically generate and send invoices immediately after completing each consulting session.
2. **Payment Reminders**: QuickBooks offers automated reminders for overdue invoices. Sarah configured reminders to be sent three days before the due date and on the due date itself, giving her clients a gentle nudge without manual follow-up.
3. **Offering Early Payment Discounts**: To encourage timely payments, Sarah offered a 2% discount for invoices paid within 15 days.
4. **Accepting Online Payments**: Sarah enabled QuickBooks' online payment option, allowing clients to pay invoices with a single click, reducing the friction of traditional payment methods.

Results:

Within two months of implementing these practices, Sarah noticed significant improvements:

- **Improved Cash Flow**: With quicker payments, Sarah had more liquidity to cover operational expenses and reinvest in her business.

- **Reduction in Overdue Invoices**: Automated reminders and online payment options led to a 40% decrease in overdue invoices.
- **Enhanced Client Satisfaction**: Clients appreciated the clear, consistent billing process and the convenience of online payments.

Takeaway: By streamlining invoicing, Sarah's firm improved cash flow, reduced outstanding receivables, and strengthened client relationships. Leveraging QuickBooks' invoicing features helped her achieve greater financial stability and focus on business growth.

Quick Tips for Optimizing Invoicing and Sales Management

- **Automate Wherever Possible**: Set up automated invoicing, reminders, and online payment options in QuickBooks to save time and encourage prompt payments.
- **Clear Payment Terms**: Make sure your invoices clearly state payment terms, including due dates, late fees, and discounts for early payments.
- **Follow Up Regularly**: Set a consistent schedule for following up on overdue invoices, using QuickBooks' automated reminders to maintain a professional, gentle follow-up.

- **Monitor Receivables**: Regularly review your receivables in QuickBooks to identify overdue accounts and proactively manage cash flow.

By mastering QuickBooks' invoicing and sales management features, you'll be able to track revenue accurately, optimize cash flow, and build lasting customer relationships. In the next chapter, we'll delve into managing expenses, providing guidance on recording and categorizing expenses, handling vendor relationships, and ensuring your business stays financially efficient.

Chapter 6

Expense Tracking and Vendor Management

Accurate expense tracking and effective vendor management are foundational to any business's financial health. QuickBooks Online provides tools for recording and managing expenses, setting up and tracking bills, and organizing vendor relationships. This chapter will walk you through the essential steps for handling expenses and vendor data, along with a real-life example that shows how controlling expenses can lead to better financial stability.

Recording Expenses and Managing Bills

Recording expenses and managing bills in QuickBooks Online keeps your books accurate and provides a clear view of where your money is going. By consistently tracking expenses, you can monitor spending patterns, ensure timely payments, and optimize cash flow.

1. Understanding Expense Types

QuickBooks Online categorizes expenses into types, such as **bills**, **expenses**, and **checks**. Knowing when to use each type is essential for accurate tracking:

- **Expenses**: These are day-to-day transactions, often paid instantly using cash or a credit card.
- **Bills**: Bills represent amounts owed to vendors and are typically paid at a later date.
- **Checks**: Checks are used to record payments made by check, including information on the check number and date.

2. Step-by-Step: Recording an Expense

QuickBooks makes it simple to record daily expenses. Here's how:

1. **Navigate to the Expenses Tab**: From the dashboard, click on "Expenses" and select "New Expense."
2. **Enter Expense Details**:
   - **Payee**: Select the vendor or payee from your list or add a new one.
   - **Payment Account**: Choose the account from which the payment was made (e.g., bank account, credit card).
   - **Date**: Enter the date of the expense.
   - **Category**: Select an expense category, such as Office Supplies, Travel, or Utilities, to help classify your spending.
3. **Add Line Items**: If the expense covers multiple categories, add separate line items with different amounts and categories for each item.
4. **Attach Receipts**: QuickBooks lets you attach a scanned or digital copy of the receipt to each expense, making record-keeping easier for tax time.

5. **Save and Close**: Once you've verified the information, save the expense to update your records.

3. Step-by-Step: Managing Bills in QuickBooks Online

For expenses that are billed by vendors and require future payment, use the **Bills** feature:

1. **Navigate to Vendors**: Click on "Vendors" under the Expenses tab.
2. **Select Vendor and Create New Bill**: Choose the vendor you're working with and click "New Bill."
3. **Enter Bill Details**:
   - **Bill Date**: The date the bill was received.
   - **Due Date**: When payment is due, based on the vendor's terms.
   - **Amount**: Enter the amount owed.
4. **Specify Expense Account**: Choose the appropriate account to categorize the bill, such as Supplies or Professional Services.
5. **Attach Supporting Documents**: Attach the bill or any supporting documentation for record-keeping.
6. **Save and Schedule Payment**: Once saved, the bill will appear in the Bills tab, and you can manage payment from there when it's due.

Setting Up and Working with Vendors
Vendors are the businesses or individuals who supply goods and services to your business.

Organizing and tracking vendor relationships in QuickBooks Online makes it easier to monitor spending, avoid late payments, and maintain good vendor relationships.

1. Adding and Organizing Vendors

QuickBooks Online's Vendor Center allows you to store essential information about each vendor, including contact details, payment terms, and notes about the relationship.

1. **Go to Vendors**: Under the Expenses tab, select "Vendors."
2. **Add New Vendor**: Click "New Vendor" to create a vendor profile.
   - **Basic Information**: Add the vendor's name, address, email, and contact phone number.
   - **Payment Terms**: Set up default payment terms (e.g., net 30) to ensure consistent payment schedules.
   - **Expense Category**: Assign a default category if you typically use the same expense category for this vendor (e.g., Office Supplies for a stationery provider).
3. **Save Vendor Details**: Save the vendor's information, and it will be available every time you need to record expenses or pay bills associated with that vendor.

2. Managing Vendor Payments

Keeping up with vendor payments is critical for maintaining smooth operations and building strong vendor relationships. QuickBooks helps you monitor due dates, track outstanding bills, and set reminders to avoid late fees.

- **Scheduled Payments**: View upcoming payment dates and set up reminders to stay on top of bills.
- **Batch Payments**: If you have multiple outstanding bills, QuickBooks allows you to process payments in batches, saving time and reducing administrative work.

Real-Life Example

Controlling Expenses for Better Financial Health

Efficient expense tracking and vendor management can lead to a healthier financial picture and a more streamlined operation. Here's an example of how one small business improved its financial health by tightening its expense tracking and optimizing vendor relationships.

Scenario: Mark owns a digital marketing agency. Over the years, he noticed that certain costs, like software subscriptions, travel expenses, and outsourced graphic design, were eating into his profits. With inconsistent expense tracking and late payments to vendors, Mark's cash flow suffered, and his relationship with key vendors began to deteriorate.

Steps Taken:

1. **Implementing Consistent Expense Tracking**: Mark began recording every expense in QuickBooks, using category tags to understand where his money was going. He attached digital receipts for each transaction, allowing him to review his spending quickly.
2. **Vendor Negotiations**: By organizing vendor details, Mark was able to negotiate better terms with suppliers. He discovered he could save 10% on design services by switching to a monthly retainer rather than a per-project payment.
3. **Automated Payment Schedules**: QuickBooks' automated reminders helped Mark pay bills on time, avoiding late fees and strengthening vendor relationships.
4. **Analyzing Spending Patterns**: QuickBooks reports helped Mark see his most significant spending areas. Recognizing that software subscriptions were a substantial recurring expense, he assessed each service's value, canceling unnecessary subscriptions and consolidating tools.

Results:

- **Improved Cash Flow**: Mark saved hundreds of dollars per month by eliminating non-essential expenses and negotiating with vendors.

- **Stronger Vendor Relationships**: Consistent, on-time payments led to better terms and the opportunity to negotiate for discounts.
- **Greater Financial Awareness**: Mark's increased visibility into his expenses helped him make strategic spending decisions, contributing to more sustainable business growth.

Takeaway: By taking control of his expense tracking and vendor management, Mark's agency stabilized its cash flow, reduced costs, and set the stage for long-term growth. Consistent expense tracking and proactive vendor management can help any business improve financial stability and build productive vendor partnerships.

Quick Tips for Effective Expense Tracking and Vendor Management

- **Automate and Organize**: Use QuickBooks' automatic reminders and category tagging to stay organized and minimize missed payments.
- **Maintain Good Vendor Relationships**: Prompt payments build trust, which may lead to favorable terms and discounts.
- **Regularly Review Expenses**: Schedule monthly reviews of your expense categories to identify potential savings and keep spending under control.

- **Keep Track of Receipts**: QuickBooks' receipt capture feature ensures you always have a record of your expenses, especially useful during tax season or audits.

In this chapter, you've learned how to record expenses, set up vendor profiles, and use these features to monitor spending effectively. As you continue, remember that managing expenses is not only about minimizing costs but also about understanding your business's financial position and making informed decisions for growth. In the next chapter, we'll look at Bank Feeds and Reconciliation, a vital process for keeping your QuickBooks records in sync with your bank statements and ensuring accuracy in your financial reports.

Chapter 7

Connecting Bank Accounts and Reconciling Statements

Keeping accurate financial records is a cornerstone of sound bookkeeping, and connecting your bank accounts to QuickBooks Online streamlines this process. By linking your accounts, you can automatically import transactions, categorize them, and perform regular reconciliations to ensure that your books match your bank statements. This chapter will guide you through linking your accounts, reconciling statements, and troubleshooting common issues.

Linking Bank Accounts and Importing Transactions

QuickBooks Online makes it easy to connect your bank and credit card accounts, allowing for seamless importing of transactions. This saves time, reduces errors, and ensures you have an up-to-date view of your finances.

Benefits of Linking Bank Accounts

- **Automated Data Entry**: Avoid manual data entry by automatically pulling transactions from your bank or credit card.
- **Improved Accuracy**: Reduce errors caused by manual input, as transactions are imported directly from your financial institution.
- **Real-Time Insights**: View your bank transactions as they happen, giving you an accurate and current picture of your cash flow.

Step-by-Step: Connecting Your Bank Account to QuickBooks Online

1. **Navigate to the Banking Tab**:
   - From the QuickBooks dashboard, go to the "Banking" or "Transactions" tab, depending on your version of QuickBooks Online.
2. **Select 'Connect Account'**:
   - Click the "Connect Account" button to add a new bank or credit card account.
3. **Choose Your Bank**:
   - QuickBooks will display a list of popular banks. You can either select from this list or search for your bank by name.
4. **Enter Your Login Credentials**:
   - Use your bank's online banking credentials to link the account. QuickBooks will securely connect to your bank.

5. **Choose Accounts to Link**:
   - Once logged in, select the specific accounts (e.g., checking, savings, credit card) you want to link to QuickBooks.
6. **Select the Date Range**:
   - Choose the date range for importing past transactions. You can typically import the last 90 days, though some banks allow for a more extended period.
7. **Review and Categorize Imported Transactions**:
   - Once connected, your transactions will appear in the Banking tab. Review and categorize each transaction to ensure they are recorded accurately.

Step-by-Step Guide to Reconciling Statements

Reconciling your bank accounts is the process of matching the transactions in QuickBooks with those on your bank statement. This ensures that your records accurately reflect your actual bank balance and helps identify any discrepancies, such as missing or duplicate entries.

Step-by-Step: Reconciling Your Bank Account

1. **Navigate to the Reconciliation Tool**:
   - In QuickBooks, go to the "Accounting" or "Banking" menu and select "Reconcile."

2. **Choose the Account to Reconcile**:
   - Select the bank or credit card account you want to reconcile.
3. **Enter Statement Information**:
   - Enter the statement's **Ending Balance** and **Ending Date** as shown on your bank statement.
4. **Compare Transactions**:
   - QuickBooks will display a list of all transactions entered during the reconciliation period. Compare each entry with the corresponding transactions on your bank statement.
5. **Mark Cleared Transactions**:
   - As you review each transaction, mark it as "Cleared" if it matches your bank statement. QuickBooks will calculate the difference between the cleared balance and the statement balance.
6. **Identify and Resolve Discrepancies**:
   - If there's a difference, review any transactions that could have been missed or entered incorrectly. You may need to adjust an entry or record any transactions that were overlooked.
7. **Reconcile**:
   - Once your cleared balance matches your statement balance (the difference shows $0.00), select "Finish Now" or "Reconcile" to complete the process. QuickBooks will save this reconciliation for your records.

Troubleshooting Common Reconciliation Issues

Occasionally, you might encounter issues that prevent your QuickBooks balance from matching your bank statement. Here are some common reconciliation problems and how to address them:

1. Unrecorded or Missing Transactions

Problem: Sometimes, transactions are missing from QuickBooks, often due to accidental omission.

Solution: Review your bank statement and check if any transactions have not been recorded in QuickBooks. Manually add any missing entries by clicking on the "+ New" button in QuickBooks and entering the missing transaction details.

2. Duplicate Entries

Problem: Duplicate transactions may appear if you manually enter a transaction and it is later imported from the bank feed.

Solution: Locate any duplicate transactions by checking for identical amounts on the same date. Delete or exclude duplicates by selecting the transaction and clicking "Delete" or "Exclude."

3. Incorrect Transaction Amounts

Problem: If a transaction amount in QuickBooks doesn't match your bank statement, this will cause a discrepancy.

Solution: Find the transaction in QuickBooks, open it, and double-check the amount. Correct any errors to match the bank statement.

4. Opening Balance Discrepancies

Problem: If your beginning balance in QuickBooks doesn't match your bank statement, it could be due to previous errors or adjustments.

Solution: QuickBooks allows you to adjust the opening balance. However, it's essential to check previous reconciliations and confirm any adjustments with your accountant, as this can impact your overall financial records.

5. Bank Fees and Interest

Problem: Bank fees or interest might not be recorded in QuickBooks, leading to a mismatch.

Solution: Enter any bank fees or interest manually in QuickBooks. Go to "+ New," select "Expense" for fees or "Deposit" for interest, and assign the appropriate category.

Best Practices for Smooth Reconciliation

Reconciling your accounts can be seamless if you follow these best practices:

- **Reconcile Regularly**: Aim to reconcile monthly to catch discrepancies early.
- **Keep Receipts and Statements Handy**: Maintaining a record of your receipts and statements will make it easier to identify errors.
- **Use QuickBooks Automation Features**: Take advantage of QuickBooks' categorization and automation tools to keep your records organized and accurate.
- **Consult with an Accountant**: For complex issues, consulting with an accountant can help ensure that your reconciliations are accurate and comply with accounting principles.

By linking your bank accounts, importing transactions, and reconciling regularly, you keep your financial data accurate and up-to-date. This foundation allows for better financial analysis, forecasting, and overall financial health. Next, we'll move into the realm of financial reporting and analysis, diving deeper into using your data to track business performance and make informed decisions.

Chapter 8

Generating Financial Reports and Analyzing Business Performance

Financial reports provide insights into your business's health, helping you make data-driven decisions to improve profitability, manage cash flow, and prepare for growth. With QuickBooks Online, generating and customizing these reports is easy, enabling you to monitor your business performance accurately and in real time.

Understanding Financial Statements: The Big Three

In QuickBooks Online, you have access to the three primary financial statements crucial for evaluating a company's performance: the **Profit & Loss Statement (P&L)**, **Balance Sheet**, and **Cash Flow Statement**. Each report provides different insights, allowing you to see where your money comes from, where it goes, and how it impacts the overall financial position of your business.

1. Profit & Loss (P&L) Statement

The **Profit & Loss Statement**, also known as the Income Statement, shows your company's revenues, costs, and expenses over a specific period.

This report tells you whether your business is profitable and how much income you have after expenses. Key elements include:

- **Revenue**: Income from sales and other business activities.
- **Cost of Goods Sold (COGS)**: The direct costs of producing or delivering your products or services.
- **Gross Profit**: Revenue minus COGS, showing the basic profitability of your products or services.
- **Operating Expenses**: Regular expenses such as rent, utilities, and payroll.
- **Net Income**: The final profit or loss after all expenses are deducted from revenue.

This statement is essential for understanding your business's profitability and identifying areas where you can reduce expenses.

2. Balance Sheet

The **Balance Sheet** provides a snapshot of your company's financial position at a specific moment. It shows what your business owns, owes, and the remaining equity. The Balance Sheet is divided into three main parts:

- **Assets**: Everything your business owns, including cash, accounts receivable, inventory, and fixed assets like equipment.

- **Liabilities**: Debts your business owes, including accounts payable, loans, and other obligations.
- **Equity**: The net worth of your business after liabilities are subtracted from assets. Also known as owner's equity or shareholder's equity, this represents the value left over for the owner.

The Balance Sheet helps you understand the financial health of your business, showing if you have enough assets to cover liabilities and how much equity you have accumulated.

3. Cash Flow Statement

The **Cash Flow Statement** details the movement of cash in and out of your business over a given period. It's essential for managing cash flow and ensuring you have enough cash on hand to meet your obligations. The Cash Flow Statement is divided into three sections:

- **Operating Activities**: Cash from regular business operations, such as sales and expenses.
- **Investing Activities**: Cash related to the purchase or sale of long-term assets, like equipment or property.
- **Financing Activities**: Cash related to funding your business, such as loans or capital investments.

This report is critical for businesses that want to keep a close eye on cash flow, manage liquidity, and avoid potential cash shortages.

Creating Custom Reports for Insights

QuickBooks Online allows you to customize financial reports to focus on specific aspects of your business. Custom reports can highlight trends, compare time periods, and track performance indicators that are most relevant to your business goals.

How to Create a Custom Report

1. **Go to the Reports Center**: From the left-hand menu, click on "Reports."
2. **Select a Report to Customize**: Choose a standard report (like Profit & Loss, Balance Sheet, or Cash Flow) that you want to tailor.
3. **Customize Report Filters**:
   - Use the customization options to select the date range, specific accounts, or columns.
   - You can filter by **location, customer, project**, or any other category that QuickBooks offers.
4. **Add or Remove Columns and Rows**:
   - If you want to focus on certain metrics, you can add columns like year-over-year comparison or remove details that aren't necessary.
5. **Save and Schedule Reports**: Save your custom report to run it anytime or schedule it

for automatic delivery to your inbox on a regular basis.

Using Custom Reports to Track Key Metrics

Some of the most useful custom reports for small businesses include:

- **Monthly P&L Comparison**: Compare profit and loss month by month to spot trends in revenue and expenses.
- **Customer Sales Summary**: Understand which customers are bringing in the most revenue, helping you focus on high-value relationships.
- **Expense Breakdown by Category**: Track where you're spending the most and identify areas for cost-cutting.
- **Cash Flow Forecast**: Use historical data to project cash flow for the upcoming months, allowing you to anticipate periods of low liquidity.

Practical Example

Analyzing Reports to Make Informed Decisions

Let's walk through a practical example to see how you might use these reports to make business decisions.

Scenario: You own a small retail business that has experienced inconsistent profits. You want to understand the cause of this variation and explore ways to improve cash flow and reduce expenses.

1. **Step 1: Run a Monthly Profit & Loss Report**
   - Generate a monthly P&L report for the past year to identify fluctuations in revenue and expenses. Upon reviewing, you notice a seasonal trend—sales increase during the holiday months but decline significantly in the summer.
2. **Step 2: Examine the Balance Sheet for Liquidity**
   - Look at your Balance Sheet to assess whether you have sufficient cash and assets to cover liabilities, especially during low-sales periods. You observe that accounts payable tend to increase during the summer months, indicating potential cash flow issues.
3. **Step 3: Review Cash Flow Statement for Operating Activities**
   - Generate a Cash Flow Statement focused on operating activities. This shows that cash outflows on inventory purchases are high before the holiday season. As a result, cash flow is strained during the summer, affecting your ability to cover expenses.
4. **Step 4: Create an Expense Breakdown Report**
   - Run a customized Expense Breakdown report to analyze spending. The report reveals that advertising expenses remain high year-round, even when sales are low.

Adjusting your marketing budget during off-peak months could help you save.

5. **Step 5: Adjust Operations Based on Findings**
   - Based on these insights, you could implement the following actions:
     - **Reduce Advertising in Low Seasons**: Lower your advertising budget in the summer and allocate more during peak periods to maximize ROI.
     - **Negotiate Vendor Terms**: Contact suppliers to negotiate extended payment terms for inventory purchases, allowing you to delay cash outflows during lean periods.
     - **Build a Cash Reserve**: Use profits from high-sales months to build a cash reserve, ensuring you have funds to cover operating expenses when cash flow dips.

This analysis not only improves your cash flow but also helps stabilize profitability across the year. By regularly reviewing and customizing these reports, you gain insights that help in optimizing both day-to-day and strategic business decisions.

Through regular use of these reports, QuickBooks Online empowers you with the data you need to run your business efficiently. From evaluating profitability to managing cash flow, these tools provide a strong foundation for sustainable growth and financial health. Next, we'll explore ways to streamline processes through automation, saving you time and reducing manual errors.

Chapter 9

Managing Cash Flow, Accounts Payable, and Accounts Receivable

Efficient cash flow management is essential for any business to stay operational and grow. Cash flow reflects the movement of money in and out of your business, impacting everything from day-to-day expenses to long-term investments. By understanding how to manage cash flow, accounts payable, and accounts receivable in QuickBooks Online, you'll be better equipped to keep your finances stable and prepare for growth opportunities.

Tracking Cash Flow and Setting Up Payment Terms

Cash flow is more than just keeping an eye on your bank balance; it's about understanding how money circulates through your business and planning for times when cash may be low.

Why Cash Flow Matters

Cash flow is critical because it affects your ability to:

- Pay bills on time

- Meet payroll obligations
- Invest in growth opportunities
- Handle unexpected expenses

A steady positive cash flow ensures that your business can operate smoothly without disruptions.

Setting Up Payment Terms to Control Cash Flow

Setting up clear payment terms for both your customers and vendors can help regulate your cash flow. In QuickBooks Online, you can specify payment terms that determine when payments are due and help avoid delays. Here's how to set them up:

1. **Define Payment Terms for Customers**:
   - Go to the **Settings** > **Account and Settings** > **Sales** > **Sales form content**.
   - Click **Edit** to set the default payment terms for invoices, such as **Net 15** (payment due in 15 days) or **Net 30**.
   - Clear terms can encourage customers to pay on time and give you a predictable schedule for cash inflow.
2. **Set Up Payment Terms for Vendors**:
   - Under **Settings**, go to **Expenses** and set default payment terms for vendors.
   - Terms like **Net 45** or **Net 60** can give you more flexibility in managing cash outflows, especially if cash is tight.

3. **Track Due Dates**:
   - Use QuickBooks reminders to keep track of due dates for both receivables and payables, ensuring that your cash inflows and outflows align with your financial planning.

Managing Receivables and Payables Efficiently

Efficient management of accounts receivable (AR) and accounts payable (AP) keeps your cash flow healthy. Accounts receivable refers to the money owed to you by customers, while accounts payable is what you owe to vendors and suppliers.

Managing Accounts Receivable

The goal with AR is to ensure timely payments from customers, minimizing the risk of overdue invoices. Here are steps to streamline your AR process in QuickBooks:

1. **Automate Invoicing**:
   - Schedule recurring invoices for regular customers to save time and ensure that invoices are sent promptly.
   - QuickBooks also allows you to add a "Pay Now" button to invoices, making it easier for customers to pay online.
2. **Monitor Aged Receivables**:
   - Use the **A/R Aging Summary** report to identify overdue accounts and focus on collections. The report breaks down

receivables by days past due, helping you prioritize follow-up efforts.

3. **Send Payment Reminders**:
   - Send automated reminders to customers when their invoices are close to due, overdue, or approaching a discount period (if you offer early payment discounts).

Managing Accounts Payable

Efficient AP management prevents late fees and helps maintain strong vendor relationships. In QuickBooks Online, you can streamline AP with these tips:

1. **Record Bills Promptly**:
   - Enter bills as soon as you receive them to get an accurate picture of your upcoming expenses.
   - Attach copies of bills to QuickBooks entries for easy reference and better organization.
2. **Schedule Payments**:
   - Schedule payments based on due dates and payment terms to avoid late fees and preserve cash flow.
   - Use the **Bill Payment** feature to batch pay multiple bills in one go, saving time and reducing the risk of missed payments.
3. **Use the A/P Aging Summary**:
   - Similar to AR, the **A/P Aging Summary** helps you see which bills are due soon. This report allows you to prioritize vendor

payments according to due dates and cash availability.

Real-World Scenario

Improving Cash Flow with Smart Practices Scenario: You run a small consulting business and often face cash flow challenges due to late payments from clients. You also find it difficult to keep up with vendor payments, which affects your credit with suppliers. To improve your cash flow, you decide to implement a few strategies within QuickBooks Online.

1. **Set Up Net 15 Payment Terms for Clients**:
   - By adjusting your default customer terms to **Net 15**, you shorten the payment window, ensuring you receive payments sooner.
   - For key clients, you add a **Pay Now** option on invoices, enabling them to pay instantly with a credit card or bank transfer.
2. **Use Automated Invoice Reminders**:
   - You activate automated reminders for invoices, so clients receive a reminder three days before the invoice is due and another on the due date. This helps reduce the number of late payments.
3. **Negotiate Net 45 Terms with Vendors**:
   - You reach out to vendors and negotiate a **Net 45** payment term, giving you more time to pay bills and improving your cash flow.

4. **Schedule Payments in QuickBooks**:
   - With vendor bills recorded promptly, you use the **Bill Payment** scheduler to make payments in batches just before the due date, allowing your business to retain cash for as long as possible.

5. **Monitor Cash Flow Using Reports**:
   - To track the impact of these changes, you use QuickBooks' **Cash Flow** report weekly. Over a few months, you notice fewer late fees, improved vendor relationships, and more consistent cash inflows.

By implementing these smart practices, you improve your business's cash flow, reduce stress around bills, and create a predictable payment schedule that keeps your business financially healthy.

Effective cash flow, AR, and AP management not only stabilizes your finances but also positions your business for growth. These practices in QuickBooks Online can free up cash that might otherwise be tied up, giving you the resources needed to invest in new opportunities.

Chapter 10

Applying QuickBooks Functions in Real-World Scenarios

QuickBooks Online is a powerful tool that goes beyond basic bookkeeping. When applied strategically, its features can enhance your business management, streamline operations, and provide insights that lead to better decision-making. In this chapter, we'll explore practical case studies that demonstrate how real-world businesses use QuickBooks for more than just balancing accounts. These scenarios will help illustrate how to apply core bookkeeping concepts to strengthen your overall business strategy.

Practical Case Studies

From Bookkeeping to Business Strategy

Case Study 1: Improving Cash Flow Management for a Small Retail Business

Business Scenario: A small boutique shop faced issues with cash flow consistency due to delayed payments and a lack of insight into expenses. The owner wanted a clearer understanding of cash flow to maintain inventory levels and pay vendors on time.

QuickBooks Solution:

1. **Automated Invoicing and Payment Reminders**:
   - The owner set up QuickBooks Online to automatically generate invoices and send reminders to customers with unpaid balances. This automation reduced the time spent chasing payments and improved cash flow.
2. **Expense Tracking and Vendor Management**:
   - By categorizing all expenses and using the A/P Aging Report, the owner could quickly see what was due and prioritize vendor payments. This helped maintain positive relationships with suppliers and avoid late fees.
3. **Cash Flow Forecasting**:
   - With regular cash flow reports and projections in QuickBooks, the business gained better visibility into when cash would be low. This allowed the owner to adjust purchasing plans and avoid potential cash shortages.

Result: Improved cash flow stability, reduced overdue accounts, and a more efficient payment process. This enabled the business to operate smoothly and invest in new inventory during peak seasons.

Case Study 2: Optimizing Time and Efficiency in a Freelance Consulting Business

Business Scenario: A freelance consultant struggled to keep up with invoices, track expenses, and manage time for billable hours.

QuickBooks Solution:

1. **Time Tracking and Billing**:
   - The consultant started using QuickBooks' time tracking feature, allowing them to record billable hours directly in the system. This integrated time tracking enabled easy invoice generation with accurate hourly charges for each project.
2. **Expense Categorization**:
   - By linking a business credit card to QuickBooks and categorizing expenses regularly, the consultant could clearly see which costs were associated with each project, making client billing more accurate.
3. **Reports for Financial Planning**:
   - Using QuickBooks' Profit and Loss Report, the consultant was able to assess which projects were the most profitable and where to focus business efforts. This insight led to strategic shifts in service offerings to maximize income.

Result: With less time spent on administrative tasks, the consultant had more time to focus on client work and ultimately increased profitability by selecting higher-value projects.

Exercises to Apply Core Bookkeeping Concepts

These exercises will help you practice essential bookkeeping skills within QuickBooks Online, reinforcing your understanding of how they apply to real business operations.

Exercise 1: Set Up and Customize Your Chart of Accounts

1. **Create New Accounts**: Set up a few basic accounts in your Chart of Accounts, including revenue, expense, asset, and liability accounts.
2. **Customize Account Names**: Tailor account names to fit your business needs (e.g., "Office Supplies" under expenses, "Client Receivables" under assets).
3. **Categorize Transactions**: Use your newly created accounts to categorize a few sample transactions.

Goal: Understand how customizing and organizing your Chart of Accounts makes your financial reporting more intuitive.

Exercise 2: Practice Creating and Sending an Invoice

1. **Create a Customer Profile**: Add a new customer to QuickBooks Online with details such as contact information and payment terms.
2. **Generate an Invoice**: Create an invoice for a product or service, adding line items with descriptions, quantities, and prices.
3. **Send the Invoice**: Use QuickBooks to send the invoice to the customer's email and track its status.

Goal: Familiarize yourself with the invoicing process, from creating to sending, and understand how QuickBooks helps you track payments.

Exercise 3: Track Expenses and Reconcile Transactions

1. **Add an Expense**: Record an expense, such as an office supply purchase, and categorize it under the appropriate account.
2. **Connect a Bank Account and Import Transactions**: Connect a bank account, import recent transactions, and match them with existing records in QuickBooks.
3. **Reconcile Transactions**: Use the Reconcile tool to ensure that your QuickBooks balance matches your bank statement.

Goal: Gain hands-on experience in recording and tracking expenses and maintaining accuracy in financial records.

Exercise 4: Generate and Interpret a Financial Report

1. **Run a Profit and Loss Report**: Generate a P&L report for the past month or quarter.
2. **Analyze the Report**: Identify key areas of revenue and expenses, and calculate your net profit.
3. **Adjust Business Strategy Based on Findings**: Consider where costs can be reduced or how revenues can be increased based on your analysis.

Goal: Develop the habit of regularly reviewing financial reports to make informed business decisions.

Practical Example

Using Reports to Inform Business Strategy

Scenario: After completing these exercises, imagine you've noticed in your Profit and Loss report that one particular product or service consistently generates higher revenue but requires more resources to deliver.

Strategic Action: With this insight, you could decide to:

- Raise prices on the high-demand product to improve profitability.
- Focus marketing efforts on this offering to increase sales.
- Streamline processes or costs related to delivering this service to improve margins.

Applying QuickBooks functions in real-world scenarios reinforces how the platform is a tool for more than just bookkeeping. By customizing, analyzing, and strategizing within QuickBooks, you're equipped to make data-driven decisions, maintain financial health, and support sustainable growth for your business. The exercises in this chapter help solidify these skills, making QuickBooks an essential part of your business strategy toolkit.

Chapter 11

Getting Started with Automation in QuickBooks Online

Automation can significantly streamline your bookkeeping tasks, allowing you to save time, reduce manual entry, and focus on what truly matters—growing your business. QuickBooks Online offers a variety of automation features, including AI-powered tools, to help you manage transactions, track expenses, and optimize cash flow with minimal hands-on involvement. In this chapter, we'll explore the basics of automation in QuickBooks and provide a step-by-step guide to setting up automation for common tasks. Finally, we'll look at a practical example to see how automation can reduce manual work and improve efficiency.

Introduction to Automation and AI-Powered Features

Automation in QuickBooks Online uses both simple rules and advanced AI (artificial intelligence) to handle repetitive tasks. This saves time, minimizes human error, and helps ensure that your books stay accurate and up-to-date. Some of the key automation and AI-powered features in QuickBooks Online include:

1. **Recurring Transactions**: Set up recurring invoices, bills, and payments for expenses that occur regularly (e.g., monthly subscriptions).
2. **Bank Rules**: Automate the categorization of transactions from your bank feed based on custom rules you set up (e.g., categorizing all payments to a specific vendor as "Office Supplies").
3. **Auto-Matching Bank Transactions**: QuickBooks uses AI to automatically match imported bank transactions with existing records in your system.
4. **Smart Invoicing and Payment Reminders**: Automatically send payment reminders to customers, reducing the time you spend on follow-ups and improving cash flow.
5. **AI-Powered Categorization**: QuickBooks can recognize transaction patterns and suggest categorizations for expenses and income based on historical data.

With these tools, you can simplify bookkeeping tasks, leaving more time to analyze reports and make strategic decisions.

Beginner-Friendly Guide to Setting Up Automations

To get started with automation in QuickBooks Online, follow these steps to set up basic automations that suit your business needs.

Step 1: Set Up Recurring Transactions

Recurring transactions are useful for payments and invoices that happen regularly, like monthly rent or client retainers.

1. **Go to Sales or Expenses**: Depending on the type of transaction, navigate to the **Sales** or **Expenses** menu.
2. **Choose "Recurring Transactions"**: Select **Recurring Transactions** under the **Settings** menu.
3. **Create a New Recurring Transaction**: Click on **New** to set up a new recurring transaction. Choose the transaction type, such as **Invoice**, **Expense**, or **Check**.
4. **Define the Frequency and Details**: Enter the frequency (e.g., weekly, monthly), start date, end date, and other necessary details. Customize the transaction by adding amounts, descriptions, and accounts.
5. **Save**: Once everything is set up, save the transaction. QuickBooks will now automatically create this transaction based on the schedule you defined.

Step 2: Set Up Bank Rules for Automatic Categorization

Bank rules help QuickBooks automatically categorize transactions that meet specific conditions, reducing manual sorting work.

1. **Go to Banking**: Click on the **Banking** tab.
2. **Create a New Rule**: In the **Banking** tab, select **Rules** and then click **New Rule**.
3. **Define Rule Conditions**: Set conditions such as the transaction type (e.g., **Money Out** or **Money In**) and add criteria for payee, amount, or description.
4. **Assign Categories**: Decide which category or account to apply for these transactions (e.g., categorize all transactions from "ABC Office Supplies" under **Office Expenses**).
5. **Save**: Save the rule, and QuickBooks will apply it to future transactions that meet these conditions.

Step 3: Use Smart Invoicing for Automated Payment Reminders

Invoicing automation saves time by scheduling payment reminders, which helps encourage timely payments from clients.

1. **Go to Sales and Select Invoices**: From the **Sales** menu, select **Invoices**.

2. **Enable Reminders**: Choose an invoice, and under **More Actions**, select **Schedule Reminder**.
3. **Define Reminder Settings**: Set when the reminder should be sent (e.g., 5 days before due date) and personalize the message if needed.
4. **Save**: Once saved, QuickBooks will automatically email reminders to your clients based on the settings you defined.

Practical Example

Using Automations to Reduce Manual Work

Scenario: Let's say you run a small consulting business. Each month, you have several clients on retainer, regular vendor payments, and a need to track expenses for office supplies and travel. You want to minimize manual entry and automate follow-ups for overdue invoices.

Automated Steps:

1. **Automating Invoicing**:
   - Set up recurring invoices for each retainer client, so QuickBooks automatically generates and sends invoices each month. This ensures your invoices are always on time and consistent.
2. **Bank Rule for Categorizing Expenses**:
   - Set up a bank rule that categorizes all transactions from your primary airline as "Travel Expenses." This way, every time you

purchase a flight ticket, QuickBooks automatically tags it as travel, saving time and maintaining accuracy.

3. **Setting Up Automated Payment Reminders**:
   - Enable payment reminders for invoices. QuickBooks will automatically send follow-up emails to clients with unpaid invoices, encouraging them to make payments on time without you needing to manually reach out.

4. **Recurring Expense for Monthly Office Rent**:
   - Set a recurring transaction for your office rent. QuickBooks will record the rent payment each month, ensuring your expenses are up-to-date without manual input.

Outcome: By implementing these automations, your consulting business can save several hours each month. Automated invoices and reminders ensure timely payments, while bank rules and recurring expenses keep records accurate and complete. Over time, automation builds an efficient financial routine, freeing you up to focus on client work and business growth.

Automation can be a game-changer for small business owners using QuickBooks Online. With simple, beginner-friendly setups, you can make bookkeeping more efficient, reduce the risk of human error, and focus on valuable business insights rather than manual data entry. QuickBooks offers a wide range of options for automation, and as you become more comfortable with its features, you'll find even more opportunities to tailor it to your unique business needs.

Chapter 12

Streamlining Tedious Tasks in QuickBooks Online

Automation is one of the most valuable tools QuickBooks Online offers, enabling you to streamline repetitive tasks, reduce errors, and focus on more strategic parts of your business. This chapter covers essential automation techniques to simplify invoicing, expense tracking, and bank reconciliations. We'll also go over tips for minimizing errors and offer a step-by-step guide to automate common bookkeeping tasks.

Automating Invoicing, Expense Tracking, and Bank Reconciliations

QuickBooks Online allows you to automate many day-to-day tasks, including invoicing, expense tracking, and bank reconciliations, making it easier to manage finances and reduce administrative workload.

1. **Automated Invoicing**: QuickBooks lets you set up recurring invoices for clients who require regular services. This ensures timely and consistent billing without the need to create each invoice manually.

2. **Automated Expense Tracking**: By connecting QuickBooks to your bank and credit card accounts, it can automatically import and categorize transactions. With custom bank rules, you can refine expense categorization, ensuring accuracy and reducing the need for manual adjustments.
3. **Bank Reconciliation Automation**: Automating bank feeds allows QuickBooks to pull transactions from your financial institutions and match them with existing records in QuickBooks, streamlining the reconciliation process and reducing the time spent on monthly balancing.

Tips for Reducing Errors Through Automation

Automation reduces errors caused by repetitive manual entry, but it's essential to set up and monitor these features correctly. Here are some best practices to keep your automated processes accurate:

1. **Define Clear Bank Rules**: Ensure bank rules are as specific as possible to avoid miscategorization. For example, setting a rule for "Office Supplies" only for transactions from verified vendors helps prevent QuickBooks from applying this category to unrelated expenses.
2. **Regularly Review Automations**: Automations can sometimes make incorrect assumptions, especially with evolving expenses.

Regularly reviewing categorized expenses and bank rules can help catch issues early.

3. **Double-Check Recurring Transactions**: Periodically review recurring invoices and expenses to ensure they reflect the latest pricing, terms, or client agreements.

4. **Enable Notifications**: QuickBooks allows you to set up email or mobile alerts for specific activities, such as when invoices are generated or payments are received. These alerts can serve as reminders to check on automated tasks and confirm they're functioning correctly.

Step-by-Step Guide to Automating Common Bookkeeping Tasks

Step 1: Automating Invoicing

Automated invoicing in QuickBooks Online ensures consistency in billing and timely follow-ups with clients. Here's how to set it up:

1. **Go to Sales**: From the **Sales** tab, select **Invoices**.

2. **Create Recurring Invoice**: Choose an invoice and select **Make Recurring** under **More Actions**.

3. **Define Invoice Settings**: Choose how often the invoice should recur (e.g., monthly, biweekly). Set start and end dates, add the client's details, and customize the description, quantity, and pricing.

4. **Enable Automatic Emails**: Check the option to email the invoice automatically to the client. You can also add payment reminders to ensure timely payments.
5. **Save**: Save the recurring invoice. QuickBooks will now handle invoicing on the schedule you defined.

Step 2: Automating Expense Tracking

Expense automation helps ensure every transaction is recorded, categorized, and reconciled accurately. Follow these steps to set up automatic expense tracking:

1. **Connect Your Bank Accounts**: Go to **Banking** and link your bank and credit card accounts. This lets QuickBooks automatically import transactions.
2. **Create Bank Rules**: Under **Banking**, select **Rules** and then **Create Rule**.
   - Define conditions, such as transaction type, vendor name, or amount range.
   - Assign a specific expense category, such as "Travel" for airline purchases.
3. **Review Imported Transactions**: Regularly review imported transactions to confirm they've been categorized correctly. QuickBooks' machine learning helps by learning from your corrections, making future imports more accurate.

Step 3: Automating Bank Reconciliations

Bank reconciliation is vital for accurate financial reporting, and automating part of this process can save you hours of monthly work. Here's how to set it up:

1. **Enable Automatic Transaction Matching**: QuickBooks will try to automatically match bank transactions with entries in your books. To review matches, go to **Banking** and check the **For Review** tab.
2. **Review Suggested Matches**: QuickBooks will suggest matches based on transaction amounts, dates, and payees. Confirm each match or make adjustments if needed.
3. **Reconcile Statements**: Each month, navigate to **Accounting** > **Reconcile** to compare bank and QuickBooks balances. Automated matching reduces the number of transactions you need to manually review, speeding up the process.

Practical Example

Using Automation to Simplify Bookkeeping

Scenario: Imagine you own a consulting business with monthly recurring clients, frequent travel expenses, and a range of vendor expenses.

1. **Automating Invoicing**: Set up recurring invoices for each client to ensure consistent billing, freeing up time otherwise spent creating

each invoice manually. QuickBooks will also send reminders to clients with outstanding balances.
2. **Automating Expense Categorization**: Use bank rules to categorize travel expenses from specific vendors (e.g., airlines or hotels) and assign them to "Travel Expenses." QuickBooks will automatically apply this rule to new transactions, ensuring accurate categorization.
3. **Automating Bank Reconciliations**: By importing transactions directly from your bank and using QuickBooks' auto-matching, you only need to review unmatched items or discrepancies each month, significantly reducing reconciliation time.

Outcome: With these automations in place, your business could save several hours each month on administrative tasks. QuickBooks handles recurring invoices and expenses, reduces the need for manual categorization, and speeds up bank reconciliations, allowing you to focus on strategic aspects of your business.

By setting up these automation techniques, you can streamline your bookkeeping, minimize errors, and free up time to focus on analyzing financial data and making strategic decisions. QuickBooks' automation capabilities are user-friendly, and as you grow more familiar with them, you'll be able to tailor these tools to meet your business's specific needs.

Chapter 13

Integrating Third-Party Apps for Enhanced Functionality

Integrating third-party applications with QuickBooks Online can significantly expand its capabilities, allowing you to streamline your business processes, improve data accuracy, and save time. This chapter provides an overview of popular QuickBooks integrations, a step-by-step guide for connecting apps, and a real-life application showing how e-commerce and payroll tools enhance QuickBooks functionality.

Overview of Useful Integrations for QuickBooks Online

QuickBooks Online supports a wide range of third-party apps across different categories, from payroll and invoicing to e-commerce and time tracking. Here's a look at some of the most valuable integrations:

1. **E-commerce**:
   - **Shopify** and **Amazon**: Sync sales data with QuickBooks to streamline income tracking,

inventory management, and customer insights.

- **Square** and **PayPal**: Automatically import transactions for seamless payment processing.

2. **Payroll and HR**:
   - **Gusto** and **ADP**: Integrate payroll data to ensure accurate employee payments and tax calculations, and to simplify compliance with payroll regulations.
   - **TSheets** (now QuickBooks Time): Track employee hours and sync with payroll to streamline timesheet approval and payment processes.

3. **Expense Management**:
   - **Expensify** and **Receipt Bank**: Capture and categorize expenses, upload receipts, and reconcile with bank statements directly in QuickBooks.
   - **Bill.com**: Manage accounts payable, automate bill payments, and sync seamlessly with QuickBooks for streamlined cash flow management.

4. **Inventory Management**:
   - **SOS Inventory** and **Fishbowl**: Keep inventory data up-to-date, automate reordering, and manage stock levels across locations, all while syncing with QuickBooks.

5. **Reporting and Analytics**:
   - **Fathom** and **Spotlight Reporting**: Create advanced financial reports and forecasts, track KPIs, and make data-driven decisions.

These integrations enhance QuickBooks' capabilities and help you automate workflows, reduce errors, and get deeper insights into your business operations.

Step-by-Step Guide to Connecting Apps

Connecting third-party apps with QuickBooks Online is straightforward, but ensuring the connection is set up correctly and that data flows smoothly requires some attention to detail. Here's a step-by-step guide:

1. **Access the QuickBooks Apps Menu**:
   - From your QuickBooks Online dashboard, navigate to **Apps** on the left sidebar. This will open the QuickBooks App Store, where you can explore and search for specific apps.

2. **Select and Authorize the App**:
   - Find the app you want to integrate, and click **Get App Now**. Review the permissions required by the app, as it will likely need access to your QuickBooks data.
   - Select the company file you want to connect to the app (if you manage multiple companies) and authorize the connection by following the on-screen prompts.
3. **Configure Sync Settings**:
   - Each app has unique settings for customizing the sync process. For example, with an e-commerce app, you might need to choose how often sales data is synced or which

accounts in QuickBooks should be used for sales, fees, and taxes.

- Set up rules or categories for specific transactions (such as mapping revenue, taxes, and shipping costs to specific accounts).

4. **Test the Integration**:
- Run a test transaction to ensure that data flows correctly from the app into QuickBooks. Confirm that transactions appear as expected in the appropriate categories and are properly recorded.

5. **Monitor and Adjust**:
- Once the app is integrated, periodically review the transactions it syncs to ensure accuracy. Check for duplicate entries, errors in categorization, or mismatched data.

Real-Life Application

Enhancing QuickBooks with E-Commerce and Payroll Tools

To understand the power of integrations, consider a business that sells products online and needs to process payroll for a small team of employees. Integrating QuickBooks with e-commerce and payroll tools can streamline multiple aspects of their bookkeeping:

1. **Connecting E-Commerce Data (e.g., Shopify)**:
   - For an online retailer using Shopify, integrating with QuickBooks allows sales data, customer information, and inventory adjustments to be automatically imported into QuickBooks. Each sale made on Shopify is recorded as an income transaction in QuickBooks, categorized by product type, with taxes, shipping fees, and discounts accounted for.
   - By syncing inventory, the business can ensure stock levels are updated with every sale, preventing stockouts or over-purchasing and keeping cost-of-goods-sold (COGS) records accurate.
2. **Automating Payroll (e.g., Gusto)**:
   - By connecting Gusto, payroll data is synced automatically into QuickBooks, with each payroll cycle recording wages, payroll taxes, and deductions as expenses in QuickBooks. Employee information, tax rates, and deductions are updated automatically, minimizing manual entry.
   - Gusto also takes care of tax filings and compliance, reducing the administrative burden and ensuring the business stays compliant with tax laws.
3. **Reconciling Transactions and Analyzing Financial Data**:
   - With these integrations, QuickBooks provides an up-to-date view of the

company's financial position, including real-time sales data, payroll expenses, and inventory values.

- QuickBooks reports now reflect accurate, comprehensive financial data, which allows the business owner to analyze profit margins, monitor payroll costs relative to revenue, and make informed decisions.

Outcome: By using these integrations, the business eliminates the need for manual data entry, reduces the chances of human error, and gains real-time insights into sales, inventory, and payroll. This setup not only saves time but also improves financial accuracy and allows the business to scale efficiently.

Integrating third-party apps with QuickBooks Online can transform how you manage your business's finances. Whether it's automating sales data, managing employee payroll, or keeping inventory up to date, these apps add powerful functionality to QuickBooks, making it an even more robust financial tool. With the right integrations, you can streamline operations, improve data accuracy, and free up time to focus on growing your business.

Chapter 14

Maximizing Efficiency in QuickBooks Online

Mastering efficiency in QuickBooks Online can save time, streamline workflows, and enhance overall productivity. This chapter offers expert tips for quicker navigation, methods to optimize system performance, and troubleshooting advice to handle common challenges.

Expert Tips for Navigating QuickBooks Quickly

Quick navigation within QuickBooks Online helps speed up tasks and maintain accuracy. Here are some essential tips for making the most of QuickBooks' interface and features:

1. **Utilize Keyboard Shortcuts**:
   - QuickBooks offers keyboard shortcuts to quickly access specific functions, which can be a major time-saver for frequent users. Here are a few valuable shortcuts:
     - **Ctrl + Alt + I**: Create a new invoice.
     - **Ctrl + Alt + W**: Write a check.
     - **Ctrl + Alt + R**: View reports.
     - **Alt + N**: New transaction (invoice, expense, etc.).

2. **Use Search and Global Search**:
   - The global search bar at the top of your QuickBooks dashboard is an effective way to find recent transactions, customers, vendors, or accounts quickly. Simply type a keyword, and QuickBooks will show relevant results across your entire account.
3. **Bookmark Important Pages**:
   - Bookmark commonly used pages (like the Dashboard, Sales, or Expenses) in your browser to avoid repetitive navigation. Many users find it helpful to create a "QuickBooks Folder" in their bookmarks for even easier access.
4. **Customize the Toolbar**:
   - The toolbar allows you to add shortcuts to frequently accessed features, like reports or bank reconciliations. Go to **Settings > QuickBooks Labs** to turn on additional features and access the toolbar customization option.
5. **Set Up Recurring Transactions**:
   - For regular invoices, bills, or journal entries, QuickBooks' recurring transactions feature is invaluable. Go to **Settings > Recurring Transactions** and set parameters to automate entries, reducing manual data entry.
6. **Leverage Batch Transactions**:
   - QuickBooks Online Advanced users can utilize the batch transactions feature to edit or delete multiple entries at once. This is

particularly helpful for bulk edits and saves significant time over individual entries.

Optimizing System Performance for Faster Results

If QuickBooks Online is running slowly, there are several strategies to improve its performance:

1. **Optimize Your Browser**:
   - QuickBooks Online runs best on Google Chrome, but you should regularly clear your browser cache and cookies to prevent slowdowns. Keeping only necessary tabs open while working in QuickBooks can also improve speed.
   - Consider enabling **incognito mode** when working in QuickBooks to ensure a fresh browser session without stored data slowing down performance.
2. **Check Your Internet Connection**:
   - A strong and stable internet connection is essential. Using a wired connection or a dedicated Wi-Fi network (if available) can help ensure that QuickBooks operates smoothly without interruptions.
3. **Close Unnecessary Browser Extensions**:
   - Certain browser extensions can interfere with QuickBooks' performance. Temporarily disable non-essential extensions while working in QuickBooks to reduce loading issues and boost speed.

4. **Update Your Software Regularly**:
   - QuickBooks Online is updated periodically. Ensure you're using the latest version, as updates often include performance improvements and bug fixes.
5. **Optimize Your Company Data**:
   - Over time, your QuickBooks data file may accumulate unused lists or older transactions. By archiving unnecessary data, you can reduce file size, which may improve loading speed. QuickBooks' **Data Cleanup** tool helps to compress and optimize data files, especially for users managing a large volume of transactions.
6. **Limit Users and Permissions**:
   - If multiple users are logged into QuickBooks simultaneously, it can impact performance. Limit users to those who need immediate access, and set permissions to restrict usage of resource-intensive features.

Troubleshooting Guide for Common Software Challenges

Even with a smooth setup, you may occasionally face QuickBooks Online issues. Here's how to handle some common problems:

1. **Login Issues**:
   - If you're having trouble logging in, ensure you're using the correct credentials and that there are no caps lock or spelling errors. If the problem persists, clearing the browser

cache or trying another browser can often resolve login issues.

2. **Bank Feed Connection Problems**:
   - If your bank feeds aren't syncing, go to **Banking > Bank Accounts**, and click **Update** to refresh the connection. Some banks may require multi-factor authentication, so check your bank account for verification requests.
   - If problems continue, disconnect and then reconnect your bank account within QuickBooks. Make sure your bank's website has no pending security alerts that might interfere with the connection.

3. **Error Messages When Saving Transactions**:
   - An error message when saving transactions may indicate a conflict within QuickBooks' cache. Try clearing your browser cache, and ensure that there are no unsaved changes in the transaction you're editing.

4. **Data Syncing Issues with Third-Party Apps**:
   - If third-party apps aren't syncing correctly, check the integration settings within QuickBooks and the app. Ensure permissions are enabled for both platforms. Disconnecting and reconnecting the app can often resolve syncing problems.

5. **Slow Performance During Peak Hours**:
   - Some users may experience slow loading times during peak usage hours. Try working

outside of these hours when possible. Additionally, disabling non-essential tabs and applications on your device can free up resources for QuickBooks to perform better.

6. **General Troubleshooting Steps**:
   - As a best practice, ensure your browser and operating system are up-to-date, as QuickBooks Online runs best on the latest software.
   - Refreshing the browser page, logging out and back in, or restarting your computer are also common troubleshooting steps that can resolve minor issues.

By leveraging these efficiency tips, optimizing system performance, and following troubleshooting practices, you can keep QuickBooks Online running smoothly, minimize time spent on bookkeeping tasks, and focus more on your business's strategic goals.

Chapter 15

Managing Inventory and Job Costing in QuickBooks Online

Efficient inventory and job costing management is essential for product-based businesses and service providers with complex projects. QuickBooks Online provides robust tools to track inventory, monitor costs, and manage projects effectively, enabling better control over finances and profitability.

Basics of Inventory Management and Job Costing

Inventory management and job costing are fundamental for businesses with physical products or extensive project-based services.

- **Inventory Management** involves tracking and managing stock levels, ordering products as needed, and valuing inventory to ensure accurate financial records. Good inventory practices reduce waste, prevent stockouts, and improve customer satisfaction.
- **Job Costing** is the process of tracking costs related to specific jobs or projects, including labor, materials, and overhead. Effective job

costing helps businesses determine the profitability of each project, enabling strategic pricing and budgeting decisions.

In QuickBooks Online, **inventory tracking** is available through the "Products and Services" module, while **job costing** can be managed by setting up projects and assigning costs accordingly. Both features enable small businesses to track costs accurately, ensure profitability, and make informed decisions.

Setting Up Inventory Tracking and Costing Systems

QuickBooks Online offers straightforward steps to set up and manage both inventory and job costing systems. Here's how to get started with each feature:

1. **Enabling Inventory Tracking**:
   - QuickBooks Online Plus and Advanced users have access to inventory management tools. To enable this feature:
     - Go to **Settings** > **Account and Settings** > **Sales** tab.
     - Under **Products and Services**, enable **Track inventory quantity on hand**.
   - After activation, you can add inventory items, track stock levels, and set reorder points.

2. **Adding Products to Your Inventory**:
   - Go to **Sales** > **Products and Services** > **New**.
   - Select **Inventory** to create an item and fill in details, such as the item name, SKU, description, cost, sales price, and initial quantity on hand.
   - Set up reorder points to receive notifications when stock is low. This helps prevent stockouts and ensures you have sufficient inventory to meet customer demand.
3. **Setting Up Job Costing for Projects**:
   - QuickBooks Online's Projects feature allows you to track revenue and expenses at the project level, making it ideal for job costing.
   - To enable Projects:
     - Go to **Settings** > **Account and Settings** > **Advanced** tab.
     - Under **Projects**, select **Organize all job-related activity in one place**.
   - To create a new project, go to **Projects** > **New Project** and fill in relevant details, such as the project name, customer, and project start date.
4. **Assigning Costs to Jobs**:
   - Once a project is created, expenses can be assigned directly to it. For instance:
     - When entering an expense, bill, or check, select the appropriate project under the **Customer/Project** field.
     - QuickBooks automatically categorizes these as project expenses, enabling

real-time visibility into the costs associated with each job.
5. **Tracking Labor Costs**:
   - If you need to include labor costs in job costing, QuickBooks Online allows you to track time using timesheets or link payroll expenses to projects.
   - Labor costs can be recorded through time tracking (found under + **New** > **Weekly Timesheet** or **Single Time Activity**) and then assigned to a project for accurate cost tracking.

Practical Example

Managing Product-Based Business Finances

Imagine a small business, **ABC Custom Furniture**, that manufactures and sells custom furniture items. They also handle specific client projects requiring unique materials and labor costs. Here's how they can use QuickBooks Online to manage inventory and job costing effectively:

- **Inventory Management**:
  - ABC Custom Furniture keeps raw materials like wood, paint, and screws in stock. They set up each of these materials as inventory items in QuickBooks Online, noting details like cost, sale price, and reorder points.
  - As they use materials, QuickBooks deducts quantities automatically, and ABC Custom Furniture receives notifications when items

reach reorder points, ensuring uninterrupted production.

- **Job Costing for Custom Projects**:
  - When ABC Custom Furniture receives an order for a custom table, they create a project in QuickBooks for that specific job. They assign all costs associated with building the table (including materials, labor, and overhead) to the project.
  - Throughout the project, they can monitor expenses to ensure they stay within budget and adjust resources as needed.
  - After completion, they review the job costing report to assess the project's profitability, giving insights into pricing strategy and resource management for future jobs.

By using QuickBooks Online to manage inventory and job costing, ABC Custom Furniture gains a clearer understanding of its expenses, inventory levels, and project profitability. This setup allows them to make data-driven decisions, adjust pricing as needed, and optimize resource allocation.

Proper inventory and job costing management are integral to running a profitable business, particularly for those with physical products or complex projects. QuickBooks Online simplifies these tasks by offering intuitive tools for tracking inventory levels, managing project expenses, and analyzing profitability. By following these steps and using the practical example as a guide, you can set up effective inventory and job costing systems in

QuickBooks Online that support strategic growth and financial stability.

Chapter 16

Payroll Processing and Compliance in QuickBooks Online

Payroll is a critical part of business operations, ensuring that employees are paid accurately and on time while maintaining compliance with tax and labor regulations. QuickBooks Online simplifies payroll processing by automating many tasks, from calculating withholdings to filing taxes. This chapter covers how to configure payroll settings, manage employee payments, and ensure compliance, with a case study on streamlining payroll for time and cost savings.

Configuring Payroll Settings and Managing Employee Payments

Setting up payroll in QuickBooks Online ensures efficient and accurate employee payments, making payroll management straightforward and error-free.

1. **Setting Up Payroll in QuickBooks Online**:
   - Go to **Payroll** > **Get Started** to begin setting up payroll in QuickBooks Online.

- Enter details about your company, such as business address, tax ID, and other required payroll information.
- Next, add your employees and enter their personal details, tax withholding preferences, pay rate, and payment method (e.g., direct deposit or check).

2. **Configuring Payroll Settings**:
   - **Payroll Schedules**: Create payroll schedules to manage when employees are paid. For example, you may choose weekly, biweekly, or monthly payroll cycles based on company policy.
   - **Deductions and Benefits**: QuickBooks allows you to set up deductions and contributions for benefits like health insurance, retirement plans, and other voluntary or mandatory deductions.
   - **Direct Deposit Setup**: QuickBooks enables direct deposit to streamline payments. To set this up, verify your business bank account in QuickBooks and gather employee bank details for secure and convenient payroll processing.

3. **Running Payroll**:
   - With employee details and payroll schedules configured, you can start processing payroll.
   - Select the payroll period, review hours worked (or use time-tracking if integrated), and check deductions and contributions for each employee.

- Review the final pay details before confirming payroll, then approve it to initiate payments.
4. **Managing Payroll Taxes**:
    - QuickBooks Online automatically calculates payroll taxes based on employee wages, tax withholdings, and deductions. It will generate the necessary tax forms and can file them electronically for added convenience.
    - You can also opt for reminders to help you stay on top of tax payments and filing deadlines, ensuring you remain compliant with payroll regulations.

Ensuring Compliance with Payroll Regulations

Compliance is essential in payroll processing. Accurate records, timely payments, and tax filings are critical to avoid penalties and protect your business reputation. QuickBooks Online helps maintain compliance by automating many of these processes.

1. **Understanding Payroll Tax Obligations**:
    - As an employer, you're responsible for withholding federal and state income taxes, Social Security, Medicare, and any other local taxes from employee wages.
    - QuickBooks keeps track of these withholdings and can file quarterly and annual tax returns on your behalf, reducing the risk of errors and penalties.

2. **Staying Up-to-Date with Labor Laws**:
   - QuickBooks Online updates regularly to incorporate changes in federal and state payroll laws, such as minimum wage adjustments and tax withholding changes.
   - Additionally, QuickBooks offers resources and notifications on labor law updates so you can stay compliant without needing to track each regulation individually.
3. **Accurate Record-Keeping**:
   - Maintaining detailed payroll records, including pay stubs, tax filings, and timesheets, is essential. QuickBooks automatically stores this information in a central location, making it easy to access records if needed for an audit or employee inquiries.
4. **Filing and Payment Deadlines**:
   - QuickBooks Online provides alerts for payroll tax filing and payment deadlines. These alerts, combined with auto-filing options, help reduce late fees and keep your business compliant with all required payroll submissions.

Case Study: Streamlining Payroll for Time and Cost Savings

Company Background: ABC Landscapes, a small landscaping business, manages a team of 15 full-time and part-time employees with varying schedules and roles. Previously, ABC Landscapes processed payroll manually, which required significant time and often led to errors. Manual calculations and paperwork also created challenges in ensuring timely and accurate tax filings.

Problem: Payroll processing took several hours every week, resulting in potential errors and frequent late payroll tax submissions. This impacted employee satisfaction and created compliance risks.

Solution with QuickBooks Online:

1. **Automated Payroll Processing**: ABC Landscapes set up QuickBooks Online's payroll system, enabling automatic calculations for each employee's hours, tax withholdings, and benefit deductions.
2. **Direct Deposit**: By switching to direct deposit, employees received payments directly into their bank accounts, reducing the administrative work involved in issuing checks.
3. **Automated Tax Filing**: QuickBooks automatically calculated and filed payroll taxes, ensuring that ABC Landscapes remained compliant without needing to track every deadline manually.
4. **Time Tracking Integration**: ABC Landscapes also integrated time-tracking software with QuickBooks Online, allowing employee hours to sync automatically with payroll, further reducing errors and time spent on manual data entry.

Results:

- ABC Landscapes cut payroll processing time by over 50%, saving several hours weekly.
- Direct deposit improved employee satisfaction as payments were consistent and timely.
- Automated tax filing reduced the risk of penalties, keeping the business compliant and stress-free.

With QuickBooks Online, ABC Landscapes not only streamlined payroll but also gained time back to focus on growing their business. Employee morale improved due to reliable payments, and management had greater peace of mind knowing that compliance was handled.

Payroll processing and compliance are critical to effective business management, supporting accurate employee payments, tax withholding, and regulatory compliance. QuickBooks Online offers automation and compliance features that simplify payroll, reduce the risk of errors, and save time, allowing you to focus on core business activities. By setting up payroll settings, understanding payroll regulations, and utilizing QuickBooks' automation features, you can optimize your payroll process and enhance operational efficiency.

Chapter 17

Budgeting and Forecasting with QuickBooks Online

Effective budgeting and forecasting are essential for businesses to plan for growth, manage cash flow, and make informed decisions. QuickBooks Online provides tools that help create, manage, and analyze budgets, as well as forecasting features to anticipate financial performance. This chapter explores how to set up budgets, use forecasting tools, and apply these strategies to drive growth.

Creating and Managing Budgets in QuickBooks Online

Budgeting in QuickBooks Online helps businesses allocate resources wisely, set financial goals, and track performance against targets.

1. **Getting Started with Budgeting**:
   - Go to **Settings** > **Tools** > **Budgeting** to access the budgeting feature.
   - You can create budgets based on income, expenses, or specific account categories, depending on what aligns best with your business needs.

- Select the fiscal year or period you want to budget for. QuickBooks allows monthly, quarterly, and yearly budget formats, giving you flexibility in tracking and analysis.

2. **Setting Budget Goals**:
   - Identify your revenue goals and expense limits to start building a budget that reflects your financial priorities. For example, set specific revenue targets for sales or allocate certain funds toward marketing or operations.
   - Take into account seasonal fluctuations if they affect your business. QuickBooks lets you customize budgets for each period, making it ideal for businesses with variable cash flow.

3. **Tracking Budget Performance**:
   - Once your budget is set up, QuickBooks allows you to monitor actual performance against budgeted figures. This helps you identify areas where you're overspending or underperforming.
   - The **Budget vs. Actual** report is a key tool that highlights any variance, helping you make adjustments to keep on track.

4. **Making Adjustments as Needed**:
   - As your business environment changes, you may need to adjust budgets to align with new goals or unexpected circumstances. QuickBooks makes it easy to modify your budget in real-time to reflect these changes,

providing a dynamic financial planning experience.

Using Forecasting Tools to Plan Financial Performance

Forecasting is the process of predicting future financial performance based on historical data and anticipated market trends. In QuickBooks, you can use budget insights to aid in forecasting.

1. **Forecasting Revenue and Cash Flow**:
   - Forecasting is particularly useful for anticipating cash flow, enabling you to ensure you have enough capital to cover upcoming expenses. QuickBooks uses your budget and past transactions to help you project future inflows and outflows.
   - Use historical sales data as a baseline and apply growth assumptions to predict revenue trends. If sales are highly seasonal, consider using the last year's data for each month as a starting point.
2. **Scenario Planning**:
   - QuickBooks allows you to create multiple budget versions for "best case" and "worst case" scenarios, helping you prepare for market fluctuations or business growth opportunities.
   - Adjust different variables (e.g., increase marketing budget, reduce operational expenses) to see how they would affect your financial performance. This practice is

especially useful in uncertain economic climates, where flexibility is essential.

3. **Reporting for Future Insights**:
   - By examining reports like **Profit & Loss** and **Cash Flow**, you can gain insights into future performance based on current trends.
   - Use these reports to make informed business decisions, like adjusting your pricing strategy or planning for future expenses.

Real-World Scenario

Using Budgets to Drive Growth

Company Background: XYZ Creative Solutions, a digital marketing agency, aims to grow by expanding its client base and increasing revenue through more diversified service offerings. However, managing cash flow and budgeting for marketing expenses has been a challenge, as they often under-allocate resources for client acquisition efforts.

Problem: The agency struggled with unanticipated expenses that affected profitability, especially during low revenue periods. They wanted a structured approach to budgeting that would allow them to set and reach financial goals, track expenses, and invest confidently in growth initiatives.

Solution with QuickBooks Online:

1. **Set Specific Budget Goals**:
    *   XYZ Creative Solutions established a revenue goal based on projected growth and set monthly budget targets for key expense areas, including marketing, staffing, and software.
    *   They created a yearly budget in QuickBooks with monthly breakdowns to track each department's spending and revenue performance.
2. **Track Budget Performance and Make Adjustments**:
    *   The team regularly reviewed the **Budget vs. Actual** report in QuickBooks to identify any discrepancies. By doing this, they quickly identified that the initial allocation for client acquisition was insufficient, prompting an increase in the marketing budget to support growth goals.
    *   They also noticed seasonal revenue patterns, which allowed them to plan for lower-income months by saving surplus funds in high-revenue periods.
3. **Use Forecasting for Strategic Decisions**:
    *   XYZ Creative Solutions used forecasting to predict future cash flow and potential growth scenarios. For instance, by using QuickBooks to analyze current client revenue and estimated conversion rates from increased marketing efforts, they anticipated a 20% increase in new clients in the next quarter.

- The team used this forecast to make strategic hiring decisions, adding more staff to support the anticipated client growth and ensuring they had the capacity to maintain service quality.

Results:

- XYZ Creative Solutions improved its financial stability, grew its client base by 25%, and saw a 15% increase in revenue within six months.
- By using QuickBooks Online's budgeting and forecasting features, they managed cash flow more effectively, allowing them to reinvest in growth areas with confidence.

Effective budgeting and forecasting are foundational for any business seeking sustainable growth. QuickBooks Online provides the tools needed to create, monitor, and adjust budgets, and to forecast financial performance, all of which support data-driven decision-making. By setting clear financial goals, monitoring performance, and using forecasts to anticipate future needs, businesses can not only survive but thrive by aligning financial planning with long-term growth strategies.

Chapter 18

Protecting Your Data – Security and Backup Best Practices

In an increasingly digital world, protecting your business data is crucial to maintain trust, secure sensitive financial information, and prevent disruptions. QuickBooks Online provides several built-in security features to help you safeguard data and ensure business continuity. This chapter covers essential data security practices, managing permissions, backup options, and tips for data recovery to keep your financial information safe and accessible.

Ensuring Data Security in QuickBooks Online

QuickBooks Online employs multiple layers of security to help protect your information, but there are additional steps you can take to further enhance security.

1. **Enable Multi-Factor Authentication (MFA)**:
   - QuickBooks Online supports MFA, which adds an extra layer of security. With MFA enabled, each login requires both your

password and a unique code sent to your mobile device.

- To enable MFA, go to **Settings** > **Security**, and select **Multi-Factor Authentication**.

2. **Strong Password Practices**:
   - Use strong, unique passwords for your QuickBooks account to minimize the risk of unauthorized access. A strong password should include a mix of uppercase and lowercase letters, numbers, and symbols.
   - Avoid using the same password across multiple accounts and consider updating your password periodically.

3. **Secure Your Devices and Network**:
   - Ensure all devices used to access QuickBooks Online are protected with security software and up-to-date operating systems. This reduces vulnerability to malware and unauthorized access.
   - Use a secure, private network when accessing QuickBooks, and avoid logging in on public Wi-Fi.

4. **Be Aware of Phishing Scams**:
   - Phishing scams often involve deceptive emails or messages designed to steal sensitive information. Be cautious about unsolicited emails or messages that ask for login credentials or contain suspicious links.
   - Always verify communication claiming to be from QuickBooks by contacting their support directly if in doubt.

Setting Up Backups and Managing Access Permissions

QuickBooks Online is a cloud-based software with automated data backups, but it's still essential to take additional precautions to safeguard your data and control access.

1. **Managing User Access Permissions**:
   - QuickBooks allows you to set specific roles and permissions for each user, limiting access to only the information and features relevant to their responsibilities.
   - To manage access, go to **Settings** > **Manage Users**. Here, you can add new users, assign roles, and set permissions for viewing, editing, or accessing financial data.

2. **Setting Up Regular Backups**:
   - Although QuickBooks Online performs automatic cloud backups, additional backups provide an extra layer of security.
   - You may use third-party backup services that integrate with QuickBooks, allowing you to schedule daily or weekly backups. These services can often save backup files to a local drive or secure cloud storage.

3. **Exporting Data for Local Backup**:
   - Regularly exporting your QuickBooks data to a local storage device ensures you have a copy in case of an internet or service outage.
   - To export data, go to **Settings** > **Export Data**, and select the data you wish to back

up, such as account information, financial reports, and transaction history.

Tips for Business Continuity and Data Recovery

Data loss or cyber-attacks can disrupt your business, but preparing a continuity plan ensures you can quickly recover and resume operations.

1. **Develop a Business Continuity Plan**:
   - Create a step-by-step plan for maintaining operations in the event of data loss, hardware failure, or cybersecurity incidents. The plan should outline recovery steps, responsible personnel, and priority tasks.
   - Regularly review and update your continuity plan to adapt to new security threats or operational changes.
2. **Test Your Data Recovery Process**:
   - Periodically test your backup and recovery processes to ensure data can be restored quickly and accurately. Conduct simulated recovery exercises to verify that all backup systems are functioning as expected.
   - Include your team in recovery exercises to familiarize them with procedures and identify any areas for improvement.
3. **Use QuickBooks Data Protection Services**:
   - QuickBooks Online's security and backup services offer extensive protection, but Intuit also provides optional data protection

services that offer enhanced encryption and recovery features.

- Explore available add-ons or consult with Intuit to see if additional services align with your business needs.

Data security is a critical responsibility for any business, especially when handling sensitive financial information. QuickBooks Online provides robust security tools, but by implementing additional precautions, setting up reliable backup systems, and preparing for data recovery, you can safeguard your data and ensure continuity for your business.

Chapter 19

Mastering QuickBooks Online – Recap and Action Plan

Congratulations! You've now developed a solid understanding of QuickBooks Online, from setting up your account and managing day-to-day financial tasks to streamlining processes with automation and safeguarding your data. This chapter will help reinforce the key takeaways from the book and provide an actionable plan to confidently apply your new skills, set achievable goals, and continue growing as a QuickBooks user.

Reviewing Key Takeaways and Best Practices

Let's start with a recap of the essential concepts and best practices you've learned throughout this guide. Understanding these fundamentals will make sure you're well-prepared for any financial management tasks that come your way.

1. **Setting Up QuickBooks Effectively**:
   - **Account Setup and Chart of Accounts**: Starting with a clean and organized Chart of Accounts allows for accurate categorization and reporting. Ensuring that your account

settings and preferences align with your business needs lays a strong foundation.

- **Customizing Settings and Preferences**: Tailoring QuickBooks to match your business operations makes it easier to navigate, manage data, and streamline workflows. Customize views, user roles, and notification settings.

2. **Managing Financial Tasks with Ease**:
   - **Invoicing and Sales**: Use QuickBooks' invoicing and sales management tools to create professional invoices, track customer payments, and manage receivables.
   - **Expense Tracking and Vendor Management**: Record expenses and vendor details accurately to maintain a comprehensive view of business spending and obligations.
   - **Bank Reconciliation**: Regularly reconciling bank accounts ensures data accuracy, improves financial oversight, and helps identify discrepancies.

3. **Streamlining Processes with Automation**:
   - **Using Automation and AI-Powered Features**: Leveraging QuickBooks' automation features saves time and reduces the risk of human error. Automate recurring transactions, invoicing, and payment reminders to keep operations running smoothly.
   - **Integrating Third-Party Apps**: Extend QuickBooks' functionality with apps tailored

to your industry, such as payroll, e-commerce, or CRM tools, enhancing efficiency and centralizing data.

4. **Monitoring and Improving Business Performance**:
   - **Financial Reporting and Analysis**: Generating and interpreting financial reports such as Profit & Loss, Balance Sheets, and Cash Flow Statements gives you insight into business performance.
   - **Cash Flow Management**: Implement best practices for managing cash flow, such as optimizing receivables, managing payables, and monitoring cash flow trends to make data-driven decisions.

5. **Security and Data Protection**:
   - **Securing Your Data**: Use multi-factor authentication, strong password practices, and controlled access permissions to secure sensitive information.
   - **Backups and Business Continuity**: Regularly export or back up your data to ensure continuity in case of unexpected disruptions, ensuring that your financial data remains intact and accessible.

Goal Setting and Building Confidence in Financial Management

Setting goals is the key to transforming your QuickBooks knowledge into ongoing business success. Define clear objectives to continuously improve your bookkeeping, streamline processes, and grow financial confidence.

1. **Identify Key Areas for Improvement**:
   - Reflect on any recurring challenges or areas where you'd like to gain more proficiency. Examples might include gaining deeper insights through custom reports, optimizing cash flow management, or integrating new apps for added functionality.
2. **Set Measurable Goals**:
   - Choose achievable goals and timelines, such as reconciling bank accounts weekly, reviewing financial reports monthly, or reducing overdue receivables by a set percentage within the next quarter.
3. **Create an Action Plan**:
   - Break down each goal into actionable steps. For example, if you want to improve cash flow, your plan might include setting up automated payment reminders, reviewing customer credit terms, and scheduling regular cash flow analysis sessions.
4. **Build Confidence Through Regular Practice**:
   - Commit to regular QuickBooks sessions—whether it's setting aside time each week to review transactions or monthly sessions to review reports and projections. Consistency will help you become more comfortable and efficient with QuickBooks.

Exploring Additional Learning Resources

Mastering QuickBooks is an ongoing journey, and QuickBooks' ecosystem offers a wealth of resources to help you continue growing. Below are some recommended avenues to keep your skills sharp and stay updated on new features and best practices.

1. **QuickBooks Help Center**:
   - QuickBooks' Help Center includes tutorials, articles, and guides covering everything from basic functions to advanced topics. This is a great place to troubleshoot or deepen your understanding.
2. **QuickBooks Training and Certifications**:
   - Intuit offers online training courses and certification programs for users of all levels. Completing these certifications can boost your proficiency and increase your credibility as a QuickBooks user.
3. **Online Communities and Forums**:
   - Join QuickBooks online communities where users share advice, ask questions, and offer support. Engaging with others can give you fresh insights and solutions to common challenges.
4. **Local Workshops and Webinars**:
   - QuickBooks and various financial organizations regularly offer live webinars and workshops. These sessions are great for staying up-to-date with new features, changes, and best practices.

5. **Financial Books and Blogs**:
   - Books and blogs about accounting, bookkeeping, and financial management can provide you with a broader understanding of business finance, complementing what you've learned about QuickBooks.

Moving Forward with Confidence

Mastering QuickBooks Online provides you with the foundation to manage your business's financial health proactively. Use this guide as a reference, set ambitious but achievable goals, and seek additional learning opportunities to enhance your skills. With time and consistent practice, QuickBooks Online will become an invaluable tool for growing and managing your business confidently. Here's to your financial success!

Bonus Materials

To help you make the most of your QuickBooks Online experience, here are some valuable bonus resources. These materials are designed to streamline your setup, provide essential bookkeeping practices, troubleshoot common issues, and support your continued learning through exclusive video tutorials and webinars.

QuickBooks Online Setup Checklist

Setting up QuickBooks Online correctly from the start is crucial for effective bookkeeping and financial management. Use this checklist as a guide to ensure you've completed each essential setup step.

QuickBooks Online Setup Checklist:

1. **Create a QuickBooks Account**
   - Sign up and choose the right QuickBooks plan for your business.
   - Set up basic information: business name, industry, business type, and fiscal year.
2. **Customize Company Settings**
   - Configure settings based on business needs (e.g., invoicing, tax settings, currency).
   - Set up multi-factor authentication for added security.
3. **Set Up Your Chart of Accounts**

- Customize account names, create new accounts as needed, and align with accounting standards.
- Ensure your Chart of Accounts reflects your business activities.

4. **Link Bank Accounts and Credit Cards**
   - Connect bank and credit card accounts to import transactions automatically.
   - Set up bank rules for categorizing recurring transactions.

5. **Customize Invoicing and Sales Forms**
   - Add your business logo, choose colors, and format invoices to reflect your brand.
   - Set payment terms, sales tax preferences, and other relevant settings.

6. **Configure Vendor and Customer Lists**
   - Import or add customer and vendor information, including contact details.
   - Organize customer and vendor lists for efficient management.

7. **Enable and Set Up Payroll (if applicable)**
   - Configure payroll settings to comply with local laws and regulations.
   - Add employee details and set up payment methods.

8. **Establish Security and Access Permissions**
   - Set up user roles and access levels for team members.
   - Regularly review and update permissions to maintain data security.

QuickBooks Online Cheat Sheet

1. QuickBooks Basics

- **Dashboard Overview**:
  - **Bank Accounts**: View balances and recent activity.
  - **Invoices**: Track unpaid invoices and overdue payments.
  - **Expenses**: Monitor spending by category.
- **Navigation Shortcuts**:
  - Dashboard: **Home Icon**
  - Sales: **Invoices, Estimates, Payments**
  - Expenses: **Bills, Vendors, Purchase Orders**
  - Reports: **Profit & Loss, Balance Sheet**

2. Essential Bookkeeping Tasks

- **Setting Up the Chart of Accounts**:
  - Go to **Settings > Chart of Accounts**.
  - Use predefined templates for common accounts.
  - Group accounts into **Assets, Liabilities, Equity, Income, and Expenses**.
- **Creating Invoices**:
  - Navigate to **Sales > Invoices > New Invoice**.
  - Add customer details and items.
  - Set terms and due dates.
- **Tracking Expenses**:
  - Go to **Expenses > New Transaction > Expense**.

- Select vendor, category, and payment method.
- **Bank Reconciliation**:
  - Access **Banking > Reconcile**.
  - Match transactions with bank statements.
  - Investigate discrepancies.

3. Generating Reports

- **Key Reports to Use**:
  - **Profit & Loss Statement**: Tracks income and expenses over time.
  - **Balance Sheet**: Displays business assets, liabilities, and equity.
  - **Cash Flow Statement**: Monitors cash inflows and outflows.
- **Creating Custom Reports**:
  - Go to **Reports > Custom Report**.
  - Filter by date, account, or transaction type.
  - Save for recurring use.

4. Automation and Efficiency

- **Automating Invoices**:
  - Create recurring invoices: **Sales > Recurring Transactions > New**.
  - Set schedule and frequency.
- **Linking Bank Accounts**:
  - Go to **Banking > Link Account**.
  - Select your bank, log in, and authorize access.
  - Categorize transactions automatically.

- **Using Rules for Categorization**:
  - ○ Access **Banking > Rules > New Rule**.
  - ○ Define conditions to assign categories automatically.

5. Tips to Avoid Common Errors

- **Data Entry**: Always double-check transaction dates and amounts.
- **Reconciliation**: Reconcile accounts monthly to catch errors early.
- **Backup**: Regularly export data: **Settings > Export Data**.
- **Permissions**: Limit user access to sensitive financial data under **Settings > Manage Users**.

6. Keyboard Shortcuts

- **Create New Transaction**: Ctrl + Alt + N
- **Search Transactions**: Ctrl + Alt + F
- **Open Help**: Ctrl + Alt + H
- **Navigate to Dashboard**: Ctrl + Alt + D

7. Common QuickBooks Errors and Fixes

- **Duplicate Transactions**:
  - ○ Use the **Banking > Excluded** tab to remove duplicates.
- **Unbalanced Accounts**:
  - ○ Check for missing entries or incorrect reconciliation.

- **Syncing Issues with Bank Accounts**:
  - ○ Refresh connection: **Banking > Update**.

8. QuickBooks Support and Resources

- **Help Center**: Access via **Help > QuickBooks Support**.
- **Video Tutorials**: Intuit QuickBooks Tutorials.
- **Community Forum**: QuickBooks Community.

This cheat sheet is a condensed guide to mastering QuickBooks Online. Keep it handy for quick reference while managing your business finances!

Bookkeeping Best Practices Cheat Sheet

Mastering bookkeeping basics is essential for keeping your financial records organized. This cheat sheet provides key practices to help you maintain accurate, up-to-date records.

Bookkeeping Best Practices:

1. **Record Transactions Promptly**
   - Enter transactions as they occur to avoid backlogs and reduce errors.
   - Use automated features like bank feeds and recurring entries for efficiency.
2. **Reconcile Bank Accounts Regularly**
   - Perform monthly reconciliations to ensure accurate records.
   - Review each transaction to match bank statements with QuickBooks.
3. **Monitor Cash Flow Closely**
   - Track inflows and outflows weekly or monthly to prevent cash shortages.
   - Forecast upcoming expenses and revenue to anticipate cash needs.
4. **Keep Personal and Business Finances Separate**
   - Avoid mixing personal and business expenses to maintain clear records.
   - Use a dedicated business account for all transactions.
5. **Organize Invoices and Receipts**

- Keep digital or physical copies of invoices, receipts, and bills for future reference.
- Use QuickBooks' attachments feature to link documents to transactions.

6. **Generate and Review Financial Reports**
   - Run Profit & Loss, Balance Sheet, and Cash Flow reports monthly.
   - Analyze financial data to spot trends, identify growth areas, and address issues.

Common QuickBooks Errors and Troubleshooting Guide

QuickBooks is powerful but not without occasional challenges. Here's a guide to resolving common errors to keep QuickBooks running smoothly.

Common QuickBooks Errors and Solutions:

1. **Duplicate Transactions in Bank Feeds**
   - **Cause**: Transactions imported more than once.
   - **Solution**: Delete duplicates and adjust bank rules to prevent future occurrences.
2. **Reconciliation Discrepancies**
   - **Cause**: Editing or deleting reconciled transactions.
   - **Solution**: Run a reconciliation discrepancy report, identify changes, and correct records.
3. **Incorrect Balance Sheet Totals**
   - **Cause**: Data entry errors or unbalanced entries.
   - **Solution**: Review transactions, particularly journal entries, and correct inconsistencies.
4. **Uncategorized Transactions**
   - **Cause**: Imported transactions not automatically categorized.
   - **Solution**: Set up bank rules for common expenses and income sources.
5. **Payroll Tax Calculation Errors**
   - **Cause**: Incorrect payroll setup or missing data.

- **Solution**: Verify payroll settings and contact QuickBooks support if necessary.
6. **Error When Connecting a Bank Account**
   - **Cause**: Bank's security protocols or temporary outages.
   - **Solution**: Try reconnecting later or contact your bank for guidance.

Access to Exclusive Video Tutorials and Webinars

To deepen your QuickBooks knowledge, access a range of tutorials and webinars created to reinforce your understanding of key topics, demonstrate real-world applications, and provide expert insights into advanced features.

How to Access Video Tutorials and Webinars:

- **Exclusive Video Library**: Enjoy a library of on-demand tutorials covering topics like setting up QuickBooks, automating tasks, and generating reports. Watch at your convenience and revisit as needed.
- **Live Webinars**: Join live webinars hosted by QuickBooks experts, where you can participate in Q&A sessions and learn about recent updates, features, and best practices.

Suggested Topics:

1. **QuickBooks for Beginners**: A complete introduction to navigating QuickBooks and setting up for success.
2. **Automating Your Bookkeeping**: How to leverage automation for efficiency.
3. **Creating Financial Reports That Matter**: Insights into generating and interpreting key reports.
4. **Data Security and Backup Strategies**: Essential steps to protect your financial data.

These bonus materials are designed to give you additional tools, support, and confidence as you continue on your QuickBooks journey. Whether you're troubleshooting an issue, refining your bookkeeping practices, or diving into advanced features, you're now equipped to master QuickBooks Online and manage your business finances effectively.

www.ingramcontent.com/pod-product-compliance
Lightning Source LLC
LaVergne TN
LVHW051344050326
832903LV00031B/3727